The Advanced Power State

Good luck Shrian.

Dave

The

Advanced
Power State

To Make You Successful in Life

David Tinney

Matador
5 Weir Road
Kibworth Beauchamp
Leicester LE8 0LQ, UK
Tel: (+44) 116 255 9311 / 9312
Email: books@troubador.co.uk
Web: www.troubador.co.uk/matador

ISBN 978 1848762 831

British Library Cataloguing in Publication Data.
A catalogue record for this book is available from the British Library.

Typeset in 12pt Sabon by Troubador Publishing Ltd, Leicester, UK
Printed in Great Britain by the MPG Books Group, Bodmin and Kings Lynn

Matador is an imprint of Troubador Publishing Ltd

Contents

Foreword

This book is dedicated to my wife Tracey and two children Mali and Aaron who are the most important people in my life. The pleasure in seeing my children grow up and develop held inspiration for me and allowed me to understand better the human psyche.

My gratitude also has to go to Sue Daniels who helped with the final editing and proofreading of the book.

How this book will help you!

This book will take you through the different tools you need and how they integrate to raise you to the Advanced Power State, a state of being that will be envied by others. As you work on each of these tools which make up the Advanced Power State, you will build up the ability to achieve your goals and be successful at whatever you want. You will also find your life will be more fulfilling.

Introduction

This book is about how to make you successful. It is my sincere belief that all you have to be is a little better than the person next door and you will shine. This book gives you the tools to make a success of yourself and thus whatever you drive yourself to do.

Like all tools, you can choose to use it properly, abuse it, or just forget it. You are the maker of your own destiny but the power of these tools and techniques, used in combination, should not be overlooked. If you are not using them then someone else will be and that means they will be a step ahead of you!

Also, like any tool, the more you practise using it the better you become. Practise enough, like driving, and you do it without the conscious mind playing a part. That should be your end goal.

In the older days a few 'special' people would be taken to certain finishing schools and taught much of the content covered in this book. You have the ability to benefit from it now.

So if you are after success then raise yourself to the Advanced Power State.

READ ON ...

Our society today takes great relish in bringing everyone down to a common denominator. This is fundamentally wrong! We should raise people to the level they can be raised to whoever they are, reward people who are effective and encourage them further. Success breeds more success.

The Advanced Power State is based on basic and sound principles. It is not rocket science! But for you to be successful at this programme there are some prerequisites:

- You must believe in yourself
- You must be prepared to change
- You must be able to take a leap of faith and even try things that you think will not work!
- You must practise and practise until you no longer have to think about what you have learned
- You must believe that the principles put forward will help you
- You must not listen to those who will try to stop you doing the programme – denigrating the ideas and sabotaging your success

There are warnings. Be prepared for the relationships around you to change as well. They may even become strained. The Advanced Power State programme is not easy; if you want easy, look elsewhere. It will take hard work and commitment, but by using these tools and developing your abilities, you will quickly see some initial rewards building to real success over time.

What makes successful people?

It is often stated that success is different for each person depending on what is important to the individual; a statement I totally agree with. Someone can be successful and have great happiness without having money.

However, most people will look at success and determine it to be about power, influence, wealth and happiness. There is nothing wrong with any of these, as long as the values contained within the person include honour, integrity and a jot of humbleness.

Part of this programme centres around a Value Based System for living and leading others. Your values and principles guide your behaviour. Just like in the fairytale where good wins over evil, it happens with people. Like people will attract like people and so evil will attract evil, but good will also attract good. It will happen with your friends and acquaintances. Successful people attract successful people. Therefore, if you change your outlook, consider that people around you are not likely to change at the same rate and it will change those relationships.

So this programme will give you the power, use it wisely! Remember the jot of humbleness!

SECTION 1

The Success Equation

CHAPTER 1

The Success Equation

There are many things that lead to a successful person, including relationships, behaviour, the ability to motivate etc. However, I have discovered that there are some basic elements for success in achieving something which, in itself, takes a person a huge step closer to overall success. This is the equation:

$$D \times E \times E(K + \chi E)T = Success$$

We will discuss the other factors in overall success later in the book.

The first thing in the equation to note is that D for Direction: this is vital. This direction encompasses vision and goal setting, and without it, you end up busy doing things well, but not necessarily in tune with what you want and/or need to be successful. Goal setting is discussed in greater detail later in this chapter.

The next two elements are E squared, or more accurately, Energy times Enthusiasm. These together, some people refer to as 'passion'. Either way, without Energy and Enthusiasm, you can be good at things and you can have direction, knowing exactly where you want to go, but ultimately you will not get out of the starting gate! There will be no momentum, nothing to carry you forward, no drive!

So where does Energy and Enthusiasm come from? Well ultimately it is only you that can affect your own energy and enthusiasm, however, others can help make this easier by assisting in motivation. In this book there will be many ideas about ways to improve not only your own E squared but, once you have started, ways to help others too.

The next two elements are 'Knowledge PLUS Experience'. Note: it is a sum not a multiplication. Experience builds knowledge, but knowledge can also be gained on its own. However, 'pound for pound' experience is more effective than knowledge on its own. This is the meaning of the small multiplier factor 'χ' on the experience 'E' in the equation. In our early years, during childhood, schooling generally gives a good proportion of our knowledge, building on it day by day. Clearly, successful people have had a good education, whether at school or elsewhere but from where do we get our experiences?

When my children were growing up, the school covered much of the education, with my wife and I helping in the evenings. However, we concentrated on giving our children experiences. I have a personal plan which I update yearly and within that personal plan I set at least ten unique experiences that my children will be given each year in order to build them.

For example, one year the experience was flying on a propeller aircraft and we had the luxury of flying on a Dakota DC 3; a great thrill for me and for my 3 year old son, as he remembered it for years and it helped to build him as an individual.

We have been on Eurostar trains, steam trains, taken walks in woods, gone to theatre productions, Mass at different churches, football matches, rugby matches at Twickenham, Disneyland, theme parks, farms, airports; the list goes on. Many parents do exactly the same thing developing their children. As a child, then, our parents help us to gain these experiences but what happens when we get older? Do we still seek different experiences to learn from or do we say to ourselves 'oh well I can never do that so that I am not going to try'?

I tried skiing for the first time at the age of 32 and I loved it – certainly a different experience.

Make a list of all the new experiences you've had in the last 10 years. What does your list tell you?

When I was younger I remember going to Beirut, before the fighting started. I was only about 7 but the visit had a big impact on my life; the traditions of the people, the natural environment, the Lords Hotel, where we stayed, the lack of fresh drinking water on tap. I still remember the stalactites and stalagmites in the Jeta grotto some 30 years later. It is not just the memories that are important. These experiences form part of the complete person I have become and therefore the judgments I make, as do all experiences and all knowledge.

Finally we have T. T is about Talent. You either have talent or you don't, and so it is in the equation.

However, I do believe that everyone has some talent at most things, even if it hasn't yet been discovered. Individuals vary in the amount of talent they have in each area but they usually have some.

The success equation will form a major part of the first section of this book. However, it would be true to say that there are other qualities that are needed for a person to be successful overall: traits such as charisma, relationships and especially the understanding of people. We should remember that almost everything you do has some kind of interaction with humans. Getting on with others is vital for success. These issues are also covered in this book.

Direction

Direction can also be classed with vision and goal Setting. Whatever it is called, it is vital for success.

Many studies have shown that the one overriding action of successful people throughout the world is the setting of goals and objectives for themselves, for anything they wish to be successful at. They also write them down and continue to review them at regular intervals. This is an understated but incredibly important element, as by writing them down you make a formal commitment to yourself. If you also share them, you make a formal commitment to those you share them with – in your conscious and your subconscious mind! Beware the power of the subconscious mind. This is an issue I'll be tackling later.

How many times have you thought about buying something and all of a sudden you start to see the item again and again? Take a car. My wife bought a Daewoo Matiz some years back. I had never seen these cars on the road but suddenly they were everywhere. I kept spotting them, some young and some old. So I had tuned my mind to make these cars relevant to my life now. They were always there, just not relevant to my life. This effect is known as 'engaging the reticular cortex'.

Once the goal is set and written down, then it is vital that you write down the steps you need to take to reach the goal: the objectives. Only a fraction of the population has goals written down. Even less have turned their goals into objectives and written those down as well. Do you want to be one of those successful people? Once the objectives have been written down, then timescales need to be added which break down the overall goal into smaller, more easily managed goals.

There will be many reasons why you may initially find it difficult to write this all down. It may be the thought that you might fail. However, successful people get over this. And anyway, so what? For anyone to be successful they need to learn from failure and just reset the goal!

The more clear your goals and objectives, the more you will desire to achieve them. Thus the more likely they will be achieved, especially if you add in the other elements of the success equation.

As with any success, personal success does not happen by accident. If you are to set goals to be successful then you have to write these personal goals down. Here is an effective way of doing it:

Put together a number of categories (and I would recommend you do this on a big piece of A3 paper in the form of a mind map). Mind Mapping will be explained later but buy any Mind Mapping book written by Tony Burzan and you will get the picture. The categories I suggest are:

- Financial
- Family

- Personal
- Education
- Work
- Spiritual
- Health

You may have others categories and feel free to use them!

Goals should be as specific as possible: for example your work category might have a branch that says you would like to reach a salary of £40,000 within 3 years, or it may be £500,000. Either way, set the goal and the timescale to achieve it.

Set clearly your goal or goals on your drawing, which you can then pin up somewhere so as to be able to continually review them throughout the year.

> *When I was 18, I set a couple of clear objectives, which at that ripe old age, I thought would probably take most of my life to achieve. I wanted to run a company and to fly on Concorde.*
>
> *I achieved both of those objectives before I was 27, flying on Concorde at supersonic speed twice before it was prematurely mothballed, and becoming a managing director of an electronics manufacturing company.*
>
> **A managing director**
>
> *I had initially believed that becoming a managing director was going to take most of my life. Nevertheless, it was something I really wanted to do.*

My career took me along several paths but I knew I would need to know about management and so I started working as an assistant in a shop. From there I worked my way up to manager before moving into different roles, and then at the age of 26, I became a managing director of a small company. I was there until a friendly buyout with a bigger company, where I remained a director of the original company and a director in the larger company. I achieved my goal! I was managing director for almost 10 years. I had a clear idea of what I wanted and this allowed me to take opportunities as they presented themselves.

Concorde was expensive and only for the rich. I was certainly not rich. However, my father worked for the airline and one of the last things he did before his sudden death was to arrange for me and my brother to go to New York on Concorde. It was an absolutely wonderful thing and an experience that will live with me forever.

Dreams can come true

Listen to *Joseph and his Technicolor Dreamcoat* and seek out the first song for the narrator where she talks about dreams coming true. It is quite powerful.

CHAPTER 2

Knowledge and Power

How the brain works

Much has been written about how the brain works and I would recommend you read a book or two on this subject. However, the key point for me in relation to extending your ability is that there is a right and a left side of the brain. The right side concentrates on art and the creative side of our life and the left on the more logical, tangible, numerical, mathematical and scientific side of life. Get these two sides of the brain working together and they are a powerful combination.

The brain – a powerful tool

I was born into a family where there were four children. We always bustled for attention and therefore I developed the ability, like many others develop, to be doing one thing and keeping an eye elsewhere. This once got me into trouble at work where I had been talking with someone quite intensely. At the same time I was obviously listening to conversations happening in the same room. In mid-conversation I broke off from talking to the person I was talking to, answered the question from the other conservation and turned back to my conversation and continued as if nothing had ever happened. It was rude and I have had to control this ability when I am around others. It is interesting to note that this ability is reduced when I am tired.

A child in the corner

A number of years back I was talking with someone and there was a child playing away in the corner. I knew and could see very clearly that the child was preoccupied with his toys. However, two hours after the conversation, the child came up with something we were talking about earlier. I was startled and I learnt a valuable lesson about talking near children.

This ability does not always come easily. It takes practice and patience.

The Brain

So I have mentioned left and right sides of the brain. The right side deals totally with images, music, art, and that kind of information, whereas the left side is analytical, dealing with logic, figures etc.

What effect does this have?

If you read the words 'motor car' you may start thinking about that Porsche you like. You can go several pages or lines of further reading without realizing you have lost concentration, or rather, redirected the concentration and are not taking in any of the words. After all, a Porsche is a sexier image than most of what you will be reading.

We have all done this and had to completely read sentences again because we had started daydreaming. Reading comes from the left side whilst daydreaming comes from the right side. The right side had very little to occupy it and so it found something to do which was completely misaligned with the reading.

This shows that the right side of your brain, the creative and imagery side is often left with huge capacity when reading. It would be excellent if we could use it more!

If you read four single words in a passage at random, you get an idea, an image.

Try it. Pick a passage of a book and read the first few words. What image do they conjure up?

The brain works on this basis of: word, word, word, which creates an image, an idea! Then more word, word, word and extended image, images or ideas, or it could be a new idea. Now eventually you get ideas that start to link to create a wider image, images or ideas.

Later in this chapter we will look at Advanced Power Reading which changes the approach to getting the brain to take in ideas and images only.

If you can get the brain to forget the words but instead create ideas more quickly and effectively, you enable your right and left sides of the brain to take in information much more effectively.

So as both sides of the brain are working, there is less chance of daydreaming. Concentration and comprehension are also increased.

The success equation states that Knowledge plus Experience are important factors. The next section is to explore how we can improve that knowledge and experience better and faster.

How to take on information more effectively

So how do you learn more quickly, whilst remembering for longer?

We have already touched on the fact that you build more knowledge from experiences than just plain knowledge. However, the way the brain works is that it 'associates' new information coming in with knowledge and experience that already exist. The more relevant background you have on a subject then the easier it is to form the associations and thus take in and remember new information.

This comes from the way the brain works in associating things with other things. You can imagine that all of your knowledge will have 'hooks' on which you can add extra knowledge. Let me explain. If I talked about stalactites and stalagmites and I explained about the pointed shape of some of them, and how they are formed over the years, without any base knowledge of the subject, then you would not really understand what I am talking about. So there are few, if any, associations that the brain can make. These ideas get left out unless we ask questions and begin to link them to existing knowledge. Improving our knowledge is therefore fundamental to success and to reaching the Advanced Power State.

So let's start with how we, as humans, take in information and how we can speed up this process.

We take on our information through our senses:

- Smell
- Touch
- Taste
- Hear
- See

There is a toddlers' programme my children used to watch called *Nina and the Neurons* which has characters for each of these five senses, having adventures and answering scientific questions as they go.

So whilst smell, touch, feel and taste are important, I am going to concentrate on the key senses that increase the intake of information most effectively: sight and hearing. To me these senses are primary to improving the speed of knowledge building.

Firstly, sight:

There are twenty times the number of optic nerves as compared with the auditory sensory area and so the optic area is really the most effective way of taking in information. Yet we use our sight and the relevant links to the brain to a very small percentage of their abilities.

The eyes see it all! But the brain does not take it all in consciously. It does subconsciously. The brain can be directed and focused to be more effective and this programme will take you through some ways to direct and focus the brain.

The brain needs to evaluate the information coming in, to think about it and process it. It then expands the initial data received by joining it with other images in your existing knowledge base and so creates new mental pathways and new images.

Observation is the first thing I would draw your attention to. The adventures of Sherlock Holmes, for me, were so important – setting up my interest with mysteries, but also giving me an insight to the importance of observation. I would sit and practice observing things just looking straight ahead, with my peripheral vision, and list all of the things I could see in the room or wherever I was. Over time, without realizing it, I became more and more observant, something that generally men do not do very well and women tend to do a lot better. Observation, however, is not the only thing! With observation, one has to continually ask the question 'Why?' Just like Sherlock Holmes would ask. 'Why are there candles in the house you are visiting?' 'What books are in the bookshelf, and why?' 'What does that tell you about the person you are visiting?' The list goes on. Read the Sherlock Holmes stories. Not only are they a good read but they focus on his ability to observe detail.

Next time you have a moment, look around you and start to question 'Why?' to every single thing you can see. Ask: 'Why are there bookshelves there?' 'Why is the window where it is?' 'Why have the people living there put terracotta curtains up?' The more you ask the questions, and deduce why, the more you find out, then the more you will build knowledge.

Also be aware of the barriers to observation:

- Stress is a major barrier
- Distraction
- Lack of concentration
- Feeling unwell (links with concentration)

Observation is important and powerful. However, taking in information through reading is still the most effective medium. It is still reckoned that 70 per cent of intake of information is done in this way. So how do we do it more effectively?

The next section will explain how. But be aware, because as stated in the introduction, the next bit will need a leap of faith. If you are not up for it then skip the rest of this chapter and perhaps the rest of the book! Maybe you're not ready for success yet!

CHAPTER 3

Advanced Power Reading

The first thing to note is that to be an Advanced Power Reader one does not need to be intelligent but able to read and understand words.

Give yourself a test and find out what speed you have for reading. I would suggest you will read about 150-300 words a minute which is absolutely fine and to be expected. Most people are around that number.

Take a book and read it for exactly one minute then go back and count the number of words. Put this down on a chart which has the week plotted against the number of words.

How fast do you think that President Kennedy could read? It was recognized that he could read in excess of 2500 words per minute. He could read all of the newspapers over the breakfast table. It was even rumoured that he would read all of the papers for the next morning's briefings in such detail that he was annoyed when others were either too tired to add to the debate, as they had been up half the night reading, or were not adequately briefed because they had not read the documents. Suffice to say that successive presidents have been given special training in this area.

So I am sure you will agree that someone has a real head start if they can read ten times faster than you. They will be able to increase their knowledge base incredibly quickly. So take a leap of faith with Advanced Power Reading.

President Kennedy was a naturally fast reader. I am not. However, I can assure you that with practice and over time, you will improve your ability to read and, what is more, your ability to comprehend and remember will be much much greater.

So why do they not teach it at school? Well firstly you need to understand what words lead to what images, and as Advanced Power Reading is actually reading sentences, you   still need to have the basic ability to read. Advanced Power Reading is then about reading those sentences much faster but in a fundamentally different way to the way we learn at school.

When we first learn to read at school we are taught to sub-vocalise the words. As most people can only talk between 150 and 200 words a minute, the result is being trained to reach this speed in reading. You need to break this link with sub-vocalisation.

Also, we are taught at school to put symbols together (letters) and form or create words, learn to interpret those words and understand them. Where they are words which create images we are also taught to form those images.

So how does the brain react to taking in these words? Well the brain has and will always take in images. So to read something is not to take in the words but to **take in the image that the words give**. I am sorry to tell you your reading speed has just dropped to about 10 images a minute!

Why? And more importantly how can you change this?

We have already suggested that words are just symbols but we read symbols. If we build the words (symbols) together we get the whole image built of the symbols. This is the same as the Egyptians who wrote in symbols. The difference is that their symbols were images in themselves and were therefore more efficient than ours, as each covered a number of words and ideas.

Learning to use images more effectively goes to the core of memory, comprehension, listening and reading. It will drastically increase the capability of your brain.

Take an example: what image does the word 'the' conjure up? The answer is it does not. It is a wasted word like 'a' and 'it'. We all know the other words like this so if we chose not to focus on these words then our images and meanings would not be impaired and yet our speed would be improved.

In the days of the caveman, communication was made by showing or by drawing, like the Greeks. Words also will always give you a disadvantage as they are only understood when you know the language. Images cross more and more barriers.

In the European Community over the last few years, look at how many signs have turned to symbols. It is now illegal to have a fire 'Exit' sign with just 'Exit' on it, it must be a running man known as 'the running Jimmy'.

Motor car buttons now all contain symbols; no longer words.

So if we are moving back to images, they are what we must be looking for in our reading.

There are a number of different courses for reading more quickly and a number of techniques based around similar principles. Advanced Power Reading draws from these principles but there are some fundamental differences which will be presented as you read on.

When I was first introduced to the concept of speed reading, I was sceptical. I felt that I could not read faster, that documents or books would just be scanned for the odd word. As my knowledge in the area grew and I experimented more, I found that although the basis was sound, it could be improved even further.

I can now assure you all: it does work. I measured my reading speed and within 6 months I had increased it to 700 words a minute, so I increased my knowledge intake capacity by three times in 6 months. As I write this book, my current rate is 1000 words a minute on easy reading material. That is approximately four times the speed at which most people can currently read. Think about what a speed increase could do for you. You will always be able to read the papers for that important meeting! Or that book that you wanted to know more from, or succeed in carrying out that research and to continue to build your Personal Knowledge Base (PKB).

You will be able to read all of your chosen journals and be right up to date.

As well as reading faster, if you do it properly, you will improve your comprehension enormously.

Ask yourself: how do naturally fast readers do it?

If you are prepared to put your scepticism aside for just a while then read on.

How to develop advanced power reading skills?

We must go back to basics. I have always hailed this core management concept above all other management tools. We will discuss this concept continuously through this book.

V.A.P.E.R:

- Vision
- Analysis
- Planning
- Execution
- Review

So the first base must be to analyse the Vision or 'purpose' behind you reading whatever you are reading. What do you want to get from this book or article?

If you are reading at school, it may be to improve your symbol (word) recognition techniques, in which case you may wish to read at a very slow, word by word basis, as we are all taught at school.

If you want to see the colours used, I can save you hours: don't read the book, just look at the pictures.

Are we there to enjoy the book? Is that our goal? Or is it to enjoy the words? If not, why are we reading the words? Is it to enjoy how the grammar is put together? If, however, it is to achieve what most people want to achieve, then it is about taking in the additional information the reading gives you.

If this is the case then it is the ideas and visual images that are the gold nuggets. Is it this gold that you want to take in? We could liken reading to gold rush miners, panning lots of dirt for those little nuggets of gold.

So the first thing to do before we pick up a book or read a document is define our vision, purpose or goal. Once we have done that we need to analyse how to achieve that purpose the most effective way i.e. with the least effort. We may want to get clues from the book itself.

Once we have done that, then we should follow the Advanced Power Reading Framework Assessment.

The Power Reading Framework Assessment covers several elements:

a) Check the Fly cover thoroughly
b) Check the contents page thoroughly.
c) Flip through the chapters as quickly as you can to pick up subheadings
d) Think about questions you want answered by what you are about to read

'a' will help you decide if you can save a considerable amount of time by not reading it at all! 'b' continues to start the hooks and the associations made by the brain. 'c', continues the process of delivering the framework hooks which will aid improved comprehension when you go to Power Read the book. 'd', the questioning will also help improved comprehension. The human condition seeks answers to questions and so you will remember things where you have asked a question far more quickly than just passive reading. Children are curious. Why should adults not be?

This covers the analysis section of V.A.P.E.R. Next we can plan the bits that will allow us to achieve our objective. After all, you may only need to read one chapter to find out what you want to meet your objective. When we have planned, we execute the reading of the article.

Once the document has been read, we then need to review the process to ensure our goal was reached. If not, we may need to start the process again.

The execution is vital. However, this improvement in reading faster does not happen overnight. It can take a considerable time. Are you willing to put in the effort?

Before going through the exercises consider the following:

Where are the pitfalls of our usual reading process?

Have you ever noticed that often, when reading, by the time you get to the end of the sentence, you have forgotten the beginning? This is because your short-term memory is not concentrating or has gone beyond its short-term memory limit, which is widely estimated to be 8 words, or things. You may also find when reading that whilst the analytical part of the brain is working, the artistic side is daydreaming. Therefore you get interrupted and forget where you started. I have read a whole paragraph and then realised that none of it has gone in because

I was daydreaming. If you increase the brain's work it has no time to daydream and retention is helped, thus reading faster actually improves retention.

When people read, they generally move their eyes down to the next line by going across the page and starting a new line, just like we used to do in typewriting in the late 20th century. Quite often you will realise you have started the same line that you read last time around as well. All of these things slow down the taking in of images into the brain. Again, the techniques in this programme will help overcome these things and you will be able to read forwards and backwards.

Distractions from the outside world are also often a reason for reducing your effectiveness. Close them out - read:

- in good light
- with a pleasant ambient temperature
- no distractions
- and somewhere where you can concentrate fully

To develop the skills of Advanced Power Readers, exercises need to be done regularly to cement the knowledge and cause it to become habit.

How to become an Advanced Power Reader

Exercises

The following exercises therefore are to help us practise, practise, practise. Remember we are undoing years of training the brain.

Before we start the exercises it is useful to carry out a little experiment to understand the work we have to do to de-train the brain. Take a book or typed A4 sheet, open it upside down and look at it for 5 seconds. Then close the book.

It is likely that you made out no words but you were aware of a pattern of paragraphs made up out of words. That would be expected.

Take another page or similar A4 sheet and look at it for 5 seconds the right way up. It is likely that your brain started to make out words. That is the way the brain has been trained to see a page and to focus in on specific symbols (words) that it recognises.

To be effective at reading we need to ensure our eyes and brain take in groups of words and paragraphs to increase the speed at which we read, so we need to practise. I suggest 15 minutes a day is a suitable time to realise the investment. However, the longer and more you practise, the faster and better you become.

So, having done some preliminary work, what is our Vision (V.A.P.E.R) for reaching the Advanced Power Reader status?

Remember: I said we have to have a purpose, goal or a vision.

You must have that goal, and really believe you *can* and *will* be able to read at 1000 words a minute, as a start, if that is your goal. If not don't bother, stop reading now and move onto the next chapter.

Next we must know where we are now, to enable us to analyse the current situation. Set yourself a reading speed objective for

3 months' time; write it down; visualise yourself achieving it.

You must, in your own mind, see yourself in 3 months' time reading at this speed. Create the visual picture in your mind- the vision must be clear. Imagine how much information and knowledge you will able to get and how that will make you a more powerful person. See yourself clearly in this place. It will be the difference between success and remaining where you are.

Remember, 15 minutes a day practice will quickly begin to make the difference.

Take an article, any article or book and read it for 1 minute. Time yourself with a stopwatch. Write down a summary of what you have read and count the number of words you have read. This should give you a good idea as to your current ability to read.

Do the same exercise with an article from the computer; some kind of word processed document.

The average reading speed is 250 and so anywhere between 150 and 300 would be considered average. Watch the average drop on the computer screen. The Advanced Power Reading exercises will help speed up computer reading too.

To finish establishing your current status, rate your comprehension. On a scale of 1-10, mark down your perception of comprehension. How much do you want it to improve by in 3 months? Again write it down and see and visualise the improvement.

I now suggest you get a sheet of graph paper and each week test your speed and comprehension. Understand where you are and how you improve.

Another exercise which I would like you to do is to hold your hands straight out in front of you and wiggle your fingers. You can obviously see those fingers wiggling. Now keep them wiggling with your eyes fixed in front of you and slowly move the fingers away from the centre. Keep your eyes looking exactly where they started ahead.(The old sausage game we all did at school.)

Do this until you lose sight of your fingers.

This is to check your peripheral vision and all but those who have an eye complaint stopping it, have the ability to use peripheral vision effectively to enhance reading. In the test your eyes will be able to see images quite far apart and if they can do that then why can they not see words at that distance as well?

The answer is: they can. Continue with the exercises and you will see how effective this can be to improve your reading speed and comprehension.

So we know where we are to start with.

More exercises

Take the room that you are in now and focus your eyes on something directly in front of you. With your eyes firmly fixed in that forward-looking fashion, note everything at the sides. List everything you can see or better still, dictate it or tell someone else to write it down for you.

This peripheral vision can be used on words but it will take practise. Practise this daily and it will, over time, improve your ability to use your peripheral vision effectively.

For 5 minutes a day you should also carry out the following exercise:

Take a newspaper column and focus in on one word in a paragraph. Keep widening you vision until you can make out every word in the line and then establish a meaning from that line. Don't forget to keep your eyes firmly fixed on the centre of the line; do not let them wander to focus in on the words.

You will find it harder to absorb words before the word you are focussed on than after the focussed word because the brain has been trained to read left to right. If you are Chinese it is the opposite direction that is more comfortable.

When the eyes wander (and trust me they will start to), then pick another line and have another go. Keep going at this. It will be frustrating but keep at it. Believe me it works!

If you do this for long enough your eyes will grow tired but it will increase your ability to take words in.

When you are at the point that this is easier to do then take two lines and slowly build up to three lines and further to full paragraphs. Remember though this is just a drill; do not try to use it to take information in at this stage. It is also another exercise that must be carried out daily if you are to retrain the brain. It will not show results immediately but keep up the effort and it will.

So once you have progressed sufficiently with newspapers, try it on books. You are the only person who can determine when you are ready. It will be harder because books have more words to a line. Make sure you use different articles and different paragraphs.

It is important at this stage not to worry about comprehension.

There are several ways of training your brain and eyes to absorb information more quickly. Try different ways until you get the most comfortable way for you. Remember: this training will lead to great results if you stick at it; results that will save you time.

How long do you spend reading in one week? Write this down and multiply by 52, now divide this by ¾. The first stage of this power reading will give you a 25% improvement, so you will save 25% of that time you have specified. What is that time worth to you? Improved time with your family, your leisure time or additional time to take in further information? It is up to you!

Firstly, when reading, make sure your environment is excellent: no distractions, good lighting, a good comfortable chair, a good temperature for you and the right height desk.

Also, some people find focussing the eyes without a guide is not easy, so use a guide if you prefer.

Use your hand or fingers. They are always with you whereas something like a ruler will not always be at your side.

Carry out this next exercise:

Use your one finger and guide it across the page, down to the next line at the end of the page and then backwards along the line. Speed up the finger going across the page to the point where it is completely blurred. Now try the exercise with two fingers; then three fingers. Your objective is to find out what you are comfortable with. It might even be that you want to use a pencil.

Remember: exercises are not part of your normal reading.

More Techniques of Advanced Power Reading

The Zinging technique

Earlier I suggested you should find out the best guide by going along the line, down and then backwards along the next line etc. Well that is the technique I call 'Zinging', basically running a 'z' pattern down a page. Remember: what we call 'reading backwards' is carried out in many countries and cultures around the world. When my son Aaron was learning to read, he would always read his numbers backwards to start with. We had to retrain him to read them in the way we read in England from left to right. So you may start with going forwards on one line and back on the next and then extend that to two lines, four lines etc. It will not happen overnight; keep working on the drills even just 5 minutes a day. The prize is worth the effort.

Read straight down a page

An alternative to the Zinging technique is to take your guide and go straight down the page in the centre, although in my experience this comes after you have mastered Zinging. Work with both and decide which one suits you. Also, there is absolutely no reason why you should not adapt these techniques to suit yourself and the material you are reading.

Reading by paragraph

As you become better at reading, using the Zinging technique or the 'straight down the page' technique, you will get to the point when this is more automatic. It is at that point that it becomes possible to extend your drills to focus on paragraphs and then go through each paragraph. Obviously this enables you to achieve very fast speeds and can take a while in coming.

As you go through these techniques, remember it is about developing the mind to accept them. Once you know them and they are automatic, then you can direct your brain to use whichever technique will be the best for you and indeed if you want to, you can slow down. The main thing is to keep working on the drills over and above your current abilities.

Remember: a muscle works on the theory of overload. Today's overload is tomorrow's achievable level. You must practise faster than you can possibly read for the brain to adjust, to be able to reach that speed. If you read slowly the brain will adapt to be even slower.

Strengthen the eye muscles

Another way to strengthen the eye muscle is to spend a few minutes of time looking at something close to the eyes and focussing on that and then focussing away. This is ideally done on a train journey where you can focus on the dirt on the screen and then on the moving trees in the distance. Your eyes will get tired after a while but that is the whole point of the training. Work your eyes to be better next time.

Challenge your speed constantly

Test yourself every month or so and keep challenging yourself with the exercises and drills introduced earlier in this chapter.

Challenge yourself with difficult to read material

Use different types of reading material, sometimes easy and sometimes difficult.

Reading newspapers and journal magazines

Newspapers always have the story in the first paragraph followed by backup information. If you do not need to read the whole article, do not read it. Read the first paragraph first and then move on.

Continue to learn vocabulary

It is worth setting a target for a word a day; that is 365 words a year. Children learn at a rate of 5000 words a year, adults at about 150. If you do an additional word a day, that would make it at around 10% of a child's rate. Of course it is in your control to do an additional number; the more words you understand, the faster you will be able to convert your understanding through Advanced Power Reading. If you see a word that you do not understand, it automatically slows you down as you need to work out the meaning through the context. Mini computers with a dictionary are a very good way to learn words. Again, with just a few minutes per day, it is worth investing in your own development. If you do not have a computer dictionary then buy a paper one which stays at your side. One warning, however: do not look up words when reading unless absolutely necessary. Work out the meaning and remember to look up the exact meaning later.

Create a brief overview of what you have read

An overview can be in any format. We will discuss Mind Mapping in a subsequent chapter, but whichever way it is done the overview helps considerably with long term retention of the information. We will be looking at techniques for this in a later chapter but it can take between 5 seconds to 1 minute to do and reaps great rewards later!

Build your background information

Not only by reading but by meeting people, talking to people, television, the Internet, by observing things, build your background information on all sorts of subjects, whether you have an interest or not. The background information will enable 'hooks', a concept to be explained later, to be more effectively and more quickly made when you power read. This will improve comprehension enormously. If you are introduced to a new subject, deliberately spend 10 minutes researching it on the

Internet after perhaps putting together a few questions to provide you with focus.

Using computers

When using a computer to read, make the screen window to the size you can screen read quickly. Newspapers have very small columns, and you can set a computer screen to simulate a column by reducing the size of the window. As your training allows, you can open up the size of the window as your ability to read larger paragraphs becomes apparent.

The basics described above will give you a start in improving your reading. If you need further support or ideas there are many books on the market that will help with speed reading and if you combine that learning with the Advanced Power Reading you will rapidly continue to improve your reading. Go with it.

Questioning

An important part of the Advanced Power Reading framework is to get your brain into questioning mode. The human condition is that it seeks out answers in a hungry fashion and you will learn and retain a lot more if they are the answers to questions you have already posed.

Remember: the most effective human beings work on achieving goals and objectives. The more you set, write down and review your goals, the more you will achieve; so this applies to Power Reading too.

Once you have been carrying out these exercises and drills for a while I would expect you to be:

1. Reading much faster
2. Comprehending more
3. Remembering much more
4. Concentrating more
5. Having less distractions
6. Linking ideas better to help build the knowledge base

It has been stated by scientists that most people's brain can process at least eight times faster than you speak or read i.e. over 2000 wpm, but memory works on association and attaching new ideas or images to existing ones, which is why your Personal Knowledge Base 'PKB' is just so important. It is in the PKB that the new ideas, images and concepts are hooked on to further increasing the PKB. The more background knowledge you have on a subject, the more chance of the 'hook', or association of the new idea taking effect and being remembered. The more you read, the more background knowledge you have. It is a happy circle as opposed to a vicious circle.

In our brains, as well as the conscious memory, there is clearly a subconscious mind which does not switch off and does not need to switch off. Think about the power you will have if you can consciously drive your subconscious. A subject we will look at later.

So for taking in knowledge, reading is the number one, followed by hearing, or more accurately listening.

CHAPTER 4

Advanced Power Listening

This chapter centres on the importance of Advanced Power Listening and how it integrates with the Advanced Power State.

It is recognised, by almost everyone I meet, that listening is very important and yet scientists say that only around 5% of people listen effectively.

The way you listen can make someone either like you or hate you without speaking even one word. It is listening that is the Power position, not talking! And yet even to this day, most people, including me, like to talk to put their point across.

By listening you can achieve greatness. You are in control.

Listening and hearing

So Advanced Power listening is the process of:

- Hearing
- Processing
- Interpreting
- Laying down of the neurons, the pathways in the brain

As with Advanced Power Reading, it is the intake of information that is so vital and the ability to trigger the memory. It is the link of idea, idea, idea. Not word, word, word.

How to listen better starts with the basic principle of 'do you really want to do it?' Do you have the 'desire' to listen? Most people I come across take listening for granted. 'Well of course I listen'. But do we? And how can we do it better?

To have the desire to listen, to want to do it, you must really care about the speaker and care about what the speaker actually says.

> *When I ran some courses for hopeful Members of Parliament, I found that when we were role playing chairing meetings, you could see they were not interested at all. They would look bored and everyone knew it. They were surprised when video footage was played back and they saw how bored they looked. It was a lesson many took forward into their careers.*
>
> *Also when meeting with politicians at receptions they would 'work the room', that is: go out to meet as many people as possible. Now that in itself is not wrong, but many would look over your shoulder and not into your eyes. They were not listening to you and it showed that they did not care about your viewpoint. They were looking at the next person they were to meet, or wondering whether there was a more important person in the room, hardly endearing you to them.*

With listening, concentration, yet again, is vital and so when someone is talking, use the time you have available to visualise a dynamic picture linked to what they are saying, to ensure you can remember and trigger the memories.

Remember the left and right sides of the brain. Use them both.

As our brain can process beyond five times faster than the fastest speaker, you have plenty of room to daydream. We therefore need to use that spare capacity to create memorable images to trigger the memory from what the person is saying.

The left side must take in the words and the right must be used to create visual images to tie the information into the Personal Knowledge Base. This will increase comprehension and retention.

When you listen, trust between people will improve. The majority of your listening is with your eyes. Remember your eyes give it all away.

So you need to understand how to speak to be able to listen better. Firstly it is accepted that communication is carried:

- 7% words
- 60% body language
- 33% tone and intonation

When someone speaks with a high pitched voice we attach more emotion to what they say.

For some months my newborn daughter reacted more to my wife's or my higher pitched voice than to my lower manly voice.

They cannot understand words at that age but they can understand emotion.

If someone is speaking and their inflection raises at the end of a sentence, the person gives the impression of a weaker speaker.

Bad pronunciation is also a no-no. It makes it harder to listen to and causes the wrong imagery. Additionally, greater concentration is needed to try to establish exactly what is being communicated.

> *When I was at university there was a lecturer. He could not pronounce some English words. For instance, for, the 'third approximation', which is a term used relating to work with atoms, engineering and chemistry, it would come out as 'the turd approximation' and for 1000 volts it would be 'a tarzan volts'. This caused much amusement but also confusion.*

So pronunciation is important and asking people to repeat things is an important part of listening.

Another technique in effectively listening is asking questions. One, because the brain works better and remembers longer when answering questions but, two, because the more you question, the more you can understand whether the speaker actually understands and is knowledgeable about the subject.

> *When I was teaching politicians I learnt to take in what was said and probe; to ask questions and confirm the knowledge source. I also had to use my own knowledge base to ensure the information I was being given was accurate.*

It is often as important to read between the words as it is to 'read between the lines'.

Culture and gestures also come into listening and to understand the culture of those you are talking and listening to is very important.

> *In the 1980s I attended a briefing at the White House in the USA and there was also a Japanese delegation there. As I spoke, they kept nodding 'yes' and agreeing to everything I said. It was only later that I discovered the nod is confirmation that they had heard what I had said; they did not necessarily agree. In their culture it does not automatically mean agreement.*

Another tip when listening is to listen for words that totally change meanings like:

* Eventually
* Maybe
* Should
* All in all
* Intention
* Most
* Yet
* For the most part
* Probably
* But

Look for implied words and repeat the pivotal word in a questioning way. Again, general questioning and 'questioning to the void', something we will look at later, can be deployed here.

We have already said that there is plenty of time to process the information. A pause at the end of their speaking creates a positive image which means the speaker feels you have listened and are considering a response.

All too often, listening is held back because whilst the person is talking, we are trying to formulate the questions we want to ask. How can we have a question until the speaker has finished? A pause after their speaking should be plenty of time to create an image related to what they have said and to think of a subsequent response.

We must not ask questions in our minds whilst listening! This may need practise, but persevere. The end results will be worth the effort.

If you are worried about forgetting an idea, write down a trigger word. You will remember that question from the trigger word.

If you listen, process and lay down visual images in the knowledge base, your comprehension will be improved, as will your long-term memory.

Another technique that I often use to reinforce my listening, especially when I am tired, is to repeat everything the speaker has said, not aloud, but in my mind, with a second delay. This process of repeating everything the person has said ensures that, if nothing else, I am concentrating on what has been said. This technique in itself transformed the way I listen and the amount I can remember.

I would recommend a book called *Listening Made Easy* by Robert Montgomery for further information and additional tips and techniques.

We have established that Knowledge and Experience are important and we have covered two major ways of improving our knowledge by reading and listening. We also know that:

- Knowledge is potential power
- Knowledge is gained from our senses

Seeing and hearing are two of the main senses.

Just these two areas will improve knowledge. In our equation (K+xE), the bit I have missed out is the experience (E) side.

CHAPTER 5

Experience

Your abilities are enormous, and grow based upon your experience, so have confidence and draw from your experiences.

Experience is every single thing you actually do, see, feel, touch or that happens to you. Experiences can be active or passive; they can be instigated by yourself or thrust upon you. Either way these experiences not only build on your Personal Knowledge Base but they help to form the person you are and will become.

Try things at least once and they will build you up as a person. Experience something and you can understand better whatever you have experienced and understand people better when they communicate or discuss the subject with you. Experience it and you will be in a strong position to have additional hooks that you can add information to in the future. Experiences are a better way of learning than reading or listening and yet most people do not seek out experiences, they let them come to them.

Make a list of ten different things you are going to do or experience this month. Perhaps pick two or even one for each of your objective groups which you defined in Chapter 1. Experience is vital; don't let others drive your experiences, drive them yourself.

Having discussed better ways of bringing in information and experience, what then is the use of bringing all of this information in, having these wonderful experiences, if we cannot remember them?

The next section therefore covers Advanced Power Memory.

CHAPTER 6

Advanced Power Memory

This chapter will cover tips and techniques which, if constantly applied, will become habitual, to improve your ability to recall things and with great ease automatically. It will give you some of the tools you need to have to cause a continual improvement in your memory to the point where a pad and paper are no longer needed.

You will be able to trigger those memories at will and recall information from years back with little effort.

Memory and Mind Mapping

In the late 1980s I did a seminar with a youth group for a small community theatre called the Nomad Theatre in East Horsley, on the subject of memory. The idea of this was to help them with remembering their lines. To start I asked them to remember five things and showed them a technique.

To this day, I have people who attended this seminar coming up to me and telling me the five things. I asked them to clear their minds and visualise.

- Their **bank** entrance or lobby

- A huge **clock** on the wall in front as they went in
- A large **rabbit** playing a large **piano** in the middle of the lobby balancing a **glass of water** on their head

This chapter is based on sound principles and basic principles of the way we think. Many famous names have worked on the mind and Tony Buzan must be one of the most authoritative. I have listened to Tony Buzan's ideas and would strongly recommend you research some of his material. It is life-changing.

Earlier in the chapter we discussed the importance of visual imagery. Take an example:

How long is a piece of string?

It is very difficult to understand exactly the image that the person asking this question is trying to convey. However, ask: how long is a piece of string which stretches from Edinburgh to London?

Can you see the difference?

Try something. Clear your mind and then think of :

'Breakfast'

What comes to mind? For some it will be bacon and eggs or whatever you had this morning for breakfast. For some it will be their favourite cereal etc. Each person may take a different meaning. It is important to remember this when you yourself are communicating. However, a vital part to remembering and triggering memories is to have clear images that can be linked to "hooks" in the brain through association of ideas.

Try this word.

'Motor car'

What comes to mind?

Again it is ambiguous and does not always lead to clear imagery for you to trigger memories in the future. Is it the motor car you drive that you are thinking of or that Ferrari that you have always wanted?

It is recognised that a key factor in memory and how the brain stores things, is by association. The brain will remember something more easily when it has made an association with another memory. If you do not make an association, it has a problem in building something from scratch, but at some point it has to have an association otherwise it is just, 'in through one ear and out through the other'.

The larger the Personal Knowledge Base you have, i.e. the more information you have, gives you a greater base onto which you will be able to 'hook' new ideas, the more likely you are to also remember the new information and be able to recall it. The more you read with the Advance Power Reading System and listen with the Advanced Power Listening and the more you experience, the more you are likely to remember and comprehend - full stop.

Interesting isn't it?

You will be able to recall every detail you take in:

- Timetables
- What you have to do

- Who knows who
- Who likes what
- Whose name is whose
- In fact anything you wish.

All without writing it down.

Just remember: the brain stores visual images – nothing more!

Consider the image/picture this next phrase gives you from the words:

'Not strawberries'.

What visual image have you had associated in your brain and what image will be retained? A lovely punnet of strawberries, perhaps one strawberry? Hang on; you were supposed to not think of strawberries.

'Do not smoke' just gives us the image of someone smoking. The government ran a heavy campaign at the turn of the century trying to get people to give up smoking. Big billboards with a cigarette on them and a red circle and line through it indicating: don't do it. What was the effect? It just reinforced smoking in people's minds because that was the image that the brain stored. It is the conscious mind that then came in and said 'Oh I must not think of that or do that'.

Positive communication and positive mindset will help the visualisation process. It will help the storing of images and the ability to trigger the memories. During my years of teaching prospective politicians, they were always taught never to use the opposition's name but to always refer to them as 'the opposition' because you reinforce the image of them as soon as you mention their name.

For the memory to work well it needs:

- Observation
- Visualisation
- Concentration
- Association
- Hooks
- Repetition

In one seminar a number of years ago, I was explaining how words are but symbols. I asked them to remember this by visualising a band playing cymbals under the Esher roundabout on the A3. Now whenever I drive over the roundabout or mention the word 'symbols' this image comes into my head.

So let's look at some practical tips and techniques with hooks.

Remembering people's names with hooks

Exercise 1

Make a list and set up 10 names as 'hooks'. Choose the names carefully. Link the 10 names you have written down to faces of people and choose popular names of the day. You can change these names as time goes by but more than likely you will want to add to those names and grow your list.

Read through and visually create these names/images after:

- 5 minutes
- 1 hour
- 1 day
- 1 week
- 1 month
- 6 months

You will never forget another name!

Every time you are introduced to someone, link their face and name with the person in your list. It works.

Learning languages using 'hooks' and linking

I found it very difficult to learn languages at school, specifically German. I could never remember whether something was neuter, feminine or masculine.

Well things started to improve when I used the 'hooks' and the linking technique by visualising whatever the word I had with the image of what it was and placing the image in a different place depending upon whether it was masculine, feminine or neuter. I used a couple of places in Surrey called Guildford and Leatherhead.

North Street   masculine
High Street   feminine
Leatherhead   neuter

You can also learn and remember telephone numbers by 'hooks' and linking. Most numbers can have a sequence created from the different numbers. For instance I had an old mobile number of 0958 213987.

I could remember it by 2+1 = 3 followed by 3 squared and -1 one for the rest of the numbers giving me:

213987

Association is a powerful memory tool.

Association exercises

Remembering telephone numbers using association:

737320

> In a seminar many years ago my brother had a telephone number I used to use to demonstrate the process. The location was in Surrey and most people knew and had driven on the Guildford Road, the A320, and so I used to ask them to visualise the image of a Boeing 737 landing on the Guildford Road - 737320. My brother was never that happy that everyone seemed to know his telephone number!

The secret with numbers, if you are not a natural with them, is that they are more powerful when they mean something to you and this is again where association and imagery comes in.

For a pin number of 5834 you could set an image of a beehive sitting on a crate up a tree with a saw cutting around the hive.

Incidentally, this is not my pin number now.

Learning words of a script

Anyone asked to speak must know the subject pretty well. When learning a script do you do it word by word or thought by thought? When learning do you think about what you are saying or is it in parrot fashion? Do you sit and draw pictures of long passages?

The memory will remember all of the words if you use association, link and visualization techniques. The images trigger the words stored in the mind.

It will be immeasurably harder to learn in parrot fashion, so use images.

If you are concentrating when the information is collected the mind will not forget it. It just needs to be triggered.

Try this experiment:

Take a book and read the synopsis. Think about the subject around it and then re-read the synopsis. Pick key words that form images from each sentence. To start, pick maybe 3 words each sentence. Eventually it should come down to one per sentence and then maybe even one per paragraph.

If you have mastered the link system then the piece of paper with this list can be thrown away.

You will now be able to link these ideas or words together and remember the whole of a passage, eventually word for word. You must, however, make sure you have full concentration when you read it!

I used association for remembering cues when I used to do some amateur dramatics. I would associate the beginning of the last sentence in the script from my cue to the first word in my own words.

So if the cue was 'it was the dustman's ability' and your follow on words were 'OK old sport' then I would imagine the dustman in an old sports car. The more absurd you make the image, the more you are going to remember it.

The example earlier of the rabbit in the bank was a little absurd but you can be very absurd in your visualization as these images stay in your mind more easily. These images can remain in your mind and so they can be very private and dynamic.

Repetition

We all know that repetition is a way of remembering things, and it still is. Abraham Lincoln used to wear a black hat. Some of you may have seen pictures of him. Accordingly to Dale Carnegie, he used to think up ideas for his speeches, put them on little bits of paper and stick them under his hat. His view was that when he came to give his speech he did not need to write it down because it had been on his brain for some time. You may laugh but it worked because every so often he laid out his ideas on a table before giving the speech and it helped create the links and ensured repetition. It was because there were no notes that people thought that he always spoke from the heart. He did, but with the ideas built up over a period of time. The point is that he would review these ideas every now and then. He knew them.

Use the following timings for repetition:

- 5 minutes
- 1 day
- 1 week
- 1 month
- 1 year
- 3 years

Another way of remembering is to use Mind Maps reviewed at night just before bed. This allows images to be burned in overnight and is an ideal way of reviewing the day as the subconscious continues processing overnight. The power and ability to use the subconscious and Mind Mapping will be covered later in the book. Using the subconscious will allow you to more than double the power of your mind overnight.

A key factor is that memory like any part of the body can be improved by using it.

Some people would say that memory is habit. I have certainly noted that the more you use it the more useful it becomes. Don't use it and you lose it!

> When I was 21 a data pad called the Psion II came out. I was laughed at for using this and teaching time management with it. Now everyone has a datapad. However, it had a serious side effect in the way I used it.
>
> I felt that as I had put the information 'away' in my PDA" then I did not need to remember it. In fact I believed that I did not need to remember anything as long as I knew how I could look up the information if needed. I was very wrong.

My memory became very lax and lost its effectiveness.

Only later when I went from virtually no memory to studying memory and experimenting with it, did I find out how effective the memory tools are to the Advanced Power State.

Touch in memory

With touch, images again come to mind. Touch can be used to trigger memories and reinforce learning. Children are encouraged to use these techniques. Touch also helps build positive and negative thinking. For instance, warm normally leads to pleasant thoughts whilst cold leads to negative thoughts – try it!

Have a warm bath and analyse your thoughts and then hold an ice cube against you and again analyse your thoughts. Negative aren't they?

We have already concentrated on eyes in the previous sections but just consider the effect colour has. Bright and cherry reds, oranges and yellows are all used in stage lighting for a warming effect whilst blues, greens or greys and black are used to denote cold and evil.

Hearing in memory

Loud noises are often negative whilst pleasant music is often positive, depending upon the type of music played and your taste in music. You can have loud motivating music or quiet classical music. Baroque music traditionally is used to extend the ability to learn and take information in.

Primacy and recency

There is something in memory known as primacy and recency. This basically says that the first thing you learn and the last thing you learn in a session are remembered far more than the bit in the middle.

If you read for any hour it will be the first and last 5 minutes that are more likely to be remembered.

It is therefore quite useful, if you want to aid memory, to do reading in bite-sized chunks so the primacy and recency kick in more often.

Many years ago when I first started training, we had an adage:

- Tell them what you are going to say
- Say it
- Tell them what you told them

This used the primacy, recency and the repetition effect to ensure that the summary information was remembered. It also had the effect of getting those in the seminar to start to ask themselves questions about the material before I got to delivering it.

> *I was once at a political dinner and our table was made up of very good friends. My brother was the guest speaker and as part of his campaigning team we had heard it all before.*
>
> *We were discussing memory and we played the following game and the speech appeared to go much faster.*

The game started with one item declared to start the process then people had to repeat the items in order and add one item at the end. This continued all around the table and started again when it got to the starting point.

Each person is 'out' when they make a mistake, miss out an item or call them in the wrong order.

Try it as a fun game.

Improving memory

In a later chapter, I will go through the importance that the body's health has to the Advanced Power State, and here, as with memory, the same thing applies. To optimise your ability to let information through to the brain and be able to assess it, you must be at one with your whole body, and all of your senses must be functioning at optimal capacity. This obviously does not occur if you are feeling unwell or have a headache.

Smell

Smell is vital. Smell can block positive thoughts. Take a flower: when you smell a pleasant-smelling flower what do you think of, negative things or positive? Try it next time your loved one gives you some flowers (you may have to prompt them to buy some) take a sniff. What comes to mind?

If you have citrus, rosemary or basil in the air it is said to be brain-friendly. Your mind is apparently opened up to a greater and more efficient input.

The Kipling Technique (or the '5 Whys' and questioning to the void)

I have already stated that questions are important but the one question which should be always on our lips is the question 'why?' 'Why this? Why that?' We know children always do this. We do it at school and with peers when young, however, we often lose this as we get older.

Ask the question 'Why?' five times and great benefit will befall you. I have made myself ask 'Why?' even when I know that it will make me look silly or stupid. However, more than often I see the relief on other people's faces when I realise they had no idea either. My stock phrase is 'I am not too bright on these things but why..?'

The '5 Whys' is linked to a technique I discovered called 'questioning to the void'. I am told it is used by the police when questioning people. The idea is if you continue to question until you can question no more, you will understand more of what the other person knows and you will understand whether they are sure of the information, or whether perhaps it is on shifting ground.

I use the technique in my interviewing for jobs. When someone tells me something, I want to know more and more, and the more I go into the detail the more I get to know them, what they can do and what they have done.

'Questioning to the void' allows you to learn and create additional 'hooks'. Without questioning to the void you are often leaving stones unturned which means you are working from assumptions and building up a picture which may not be quite accurate.

The power of learning

If you are reading this book it is my expectation that you will appreciate the 'power of learning'. There are some additional ways of learning that successful people use. The first to note is that 'success comes from defeat', if you learn from the defeat.

Success from defeat by learning

Each defeat, if learned from, is a step up the ladder of success. Remember: it is only by learning that we succeed anyway. Defeat is a positive reinforcer, or negative if we let it. Use it as a positive reinforcer and you will gain more from those valuable experiences.

> *A sales trainer I knew told me that as well as getting sales, each 'No' they received, they should learn from and understand the reason why they did not get the sale. His view was that if they learned something each time they received a negative response they would be more capable of converting the next client.*

So maybe a salesman should go out and say 'I want 10 "Yes" answers and 200 "No" answers and I am not coming home till I have them.' So you may have got your 'Yes' answers but not your 'No' answers. Does this mean you should carry on until you have your quota of 'No' answers? What have you learnt from those 'No' answers?

Don't let success be a step down the ladder. Do not fear failure but understand how in future you can make a success from the failure.

The actual experience, especially in defeat, will allow you to remember it so much more vividly.

Lifelong Learner

Make sure you become a 'Lifelong'.

We have enormous potential and naturally process all information and store it deep down in our subconscious. It is a natural function to process this information. We have to do it. The more we do it the more success we have and the more positive we feel. Even when school and college are over keep the mental acuity and set yourself a learning target each year.

If you fail to do this, you will fall into decline and a negative mindset. The world is changing faster than we can imagine. We need to be up to date and learning faster than it is moving on.

Be positive, feel positive, and feel fit and healthy.

In this world, information is doubling faster and faster than ever before. Do you want to be left behind? Staying still is being left behind.

The final part of the success equation is talent.

Talent

Talent is one of those things you either have or you do not. You are born with different degrees of talent for different things. Nature may change those talents but I believe they are out of your control. Sure, if you find things you want to be successful at, using the areas where you have most talent, then that is fantastic. However, talent is either there or not, it is a constant! Use the rest of the success equation to exploit those talents where possible.

SECTION 2
People

CHAPTER 7

The People Factor

Getting on with people

Somebody once told me that everything you do, everything you want, involves another person. Well whilst I do not believe it to be totally true, it is clear to me that, in the past, many more people were dependent on others, whereas now I would say most people have interdependencies on each other. People relationships are critical for success, whether that is the ability to mediate, compromise, influence, be diplomatic etc. Working with people is paramount for overall success.

This chapter will explain what I call 'Advanced Power Relations' and go through how to get the most out of the relationships you currently have, their importance and how to nurture and build relationships.

Advanced Power Relations can really only be achieved by experience. I can discuss many of the ways to get more out of relationships but in life you can learn maths and science and it is right or wrong. With people it is different. That is because everyone is unique and thinks with unique thoughts and images. There are usually no rights and no wrongs, just 'shades of grey'.

You can learn some of the basic rules but really the only way to learn is by doing, by meeting people and by experiencing people. So put yourself in the position of going out and meeting people and trying some of the techniques discussed here. Another leap of faith is required, because you must be willing to try and succeed but also to try and fail and to learn from the subsequent failure. However, it is harder to fail with relationships than it is in a maths or science test.

Perfect the way you deal with relations and you will be well on your way to achieving great things. As you go on your way and interact with others generally, analyse day by day what you do and the reaction it has on others.

To start with, there are some key things to note generally about people:

- Happy and cheerful people will be liked more than unhappy people
- People like to be involved to feel belonging and to be asked
- People like to be appreciated and thanked for what they have done
- People do not like to be vulnerable or threatened and often prefer humble people
- People do not like arguments and prefer people who are agreeable
- We all sometimes expect too much from people judging them on our own set of values and abilities
- People like genuine and honest people who do things from a good set of values, from their heart

Happy and cheerful people will be liked more than unhappy people

Whenever you see someone who is happy and cheerful, someone who has a pleasant personality, then you will naturally be drawn to them. They will be the people laughing and having fun. They will be the people who have a group around them listening to them.

If someone is happy and smiling you will feel more open to talk to them, to go up and negotiate more openly, to be friendly with them.

So when we are tired and stressed, how do we make ourselves happy? The secret is to smile, even if you don't feel like it. There is a condition that says if you smile, eventually your head will lift to join your face. So why stop there? Not only is it recognised that a glum face leads to a glum outlook but also unhappy people tend to look at the ground more. So smile in your face and lift your head. Both of these actions have the effect of taking you from being sad to happy.

Try it next time you feel sad or under the weather. Smile and keep smiling and within 30 minutes you will have lifted yourself out of your gloom.

People like to be involved, to feel belonging and to be asked

There is a famous management guru, called Maslow who developed the 'Maslow's Needs Theory', something still taught in most colleges even today. One of his needs levels was that people need to be involved, they need to belong.

If you involve people and make them feel the belonging then generally the results will always be better than leaving them out until they have to be involved. Always feel free to ask people. I used to be involved in politics and carried out something called 'canvassing'. This meant asking people how they would vote. Some people did not want to say but, with the majority of people you could see the pride in their face (except of course the cynics) when you wanted to know what they thought. Watch someone's reaction next time you ask them about something when they are not expecting it. People like to be asked.

People like to be appreciated and thanked for what they have done

In all my years of working, one thing that is often missing in people relationships, management and leadership is appreciation for a job well done. Always thank people. People like to be thanked. It isn't the courteous 'thanks' which I am referring to, it is the heartfelt, special, out-of-your-way thank you. We live very busy lives and it is difficult to remember. However, it is vital in terms of continuing good relationships.

When I was in my twenties I held a games party at my house. Once the party had finished, for some reason a couple of ladies stayed around and ended up watching 'Take That in Berlin' until 2am. Everyone else left at 12.30am. But let me tell you, the next day I found a message on my answering machine from Sarah, one of the girls, saying how much she enjoyed the evening; it was the most fun she had had for a long time and she hoped they hadn't inconvenienced me by staying on but she really had grown to love 'Take That'.

That genuine 'thank you' was a real pleasure to receive.

I experienced another example when I ran my own manufacturing company.

> A *new employee called Stephen joined the company in the production line. However, he appeared good and positive and was put on a telephone skills course very quickly to act as backup for customers calling in. He borrowed one of our cars to go to the course. He telephoned at the end of the course to ask if he could keep the car until tomorrow because he needed to go straight to his evening class and then he struck gold. He said 'thank you' for putting him on the course; it was great and he had learned a lot.*

> *That was the first person who gave me a genuine 'thank you' within the work environment for putting him on a training course, something that I do all of the time. I remember the thanks to this day. It made me feel good.*

People like humble people who admit sometimes they are wrong.

The Advanced Power State will raise you to a high place that some people only dream of getting to and so as you get there you must make sure that you continue in a humble manner. As your confidence grows, so arrogance can set in. Indeed sometimes the dividing line between arrogance and confidence can be difficult to establish but as you have confidence you will need to learn to be humble, to admit you are wrong.

In my youth there was a television programme called 'Happy Days'. There was a character called 'The Fonz' and he was a little like Danny in 'Grease'. He was cool! One episode has always stood out in my mind and that was where 'The Fonz' was wrong about something and he could not say the word 'wrong'.

The comedy line went 'OK Richie, I was wr... I was W... I was Wr..."

We are all wrong sometimes. It is only our lack of confidence and lack of self-esteem that stops us admitting it.

If you are wrong, admit it quickly and emphatically. Take the consequences for being wrong and draw lessons from being wrong. If need be, share the lessons you have taken and be humble. Say things such as 'OK, I will try to do better next time'.

People do not like arguments and prefer people who are agreeable

Time after time I see people arguing; I used to do it myself. Arguing is distinctly different from a discussion. Arguing is usually heated. To me, discussion is about bringing minds together and arguing does the exact opposite. The saying is true: no one wins an argument. I would add to this 'except the person that walks away from the argument in the first place'.

If you want to get on with someone, avoid the argument.

I have heard many people say things like 'they won the argument'; 'after I had finished they realised that they were wrong'; 'they won't doubt me next time'. Well it is unlikely they will come anywhere near them next time, unless they have to because, like negotiation, (which we will cover in depth in a later chapter) you need both parties to part as winners. Someone who has been crushed by your superior argument and your shouting will not feel like a winner. So you both lose. In addition, they will remember you long after the reason for the argument has been forgotten and it won't be because they like you.

People like to feel worthwhile and for someone to agree with you is an important part of the relationship, so be agreeable! Agree with things people say! Create a language of agreeing and if there is a time when you really cannot agree, do it nicely and agree to differ!

We all sometimes expect too much from people judging them on our own set of values and abilities

When I was 18 I read a book called *How to Win Friends and Influence People* by Dale Carnegie. Anyone wanting to understand people and get on better with them should read it. Within the book there is a passage called 'Father Forgets'. At 18 it was powerful, when I became a dad it was essential. The passage is very moving and explains how we sometimes expect too much from people.

My wife is often saying that I am always making excuses for people when they do things and so I am, because I do not want to fall into the trap of expecting more than someone can give. Others have not gained the knowledge I have, they have not the skills I have learned, they have not had the experiences, and so who am I to expect people to do, think or say what I would say? I am sure there are many people saying the same about me when I do things.

It is easy to expect others to be able to perform or to be able to do things that we can, but realise that as you grow in the Advanced Power State, people will appear to fall behind and they will appear able to achieve less and less. It is not that they are achieving less, it is that as you speed ahead you are achieving more. So do not think badly of anyone, think of how you may be able to help them, and when you come across people who are better than you, learn from them and develop yourself further.

People like genuine and honest people who do things from a good set of values; from the heart

I was at a theatre show in the West End called 'Time – the Musical'. From this I gathered an important lesson in life that has stood the test of time: 'If your heart is in order then your thinking will be in order' and if your thinking is in order then your words will be in order and you do not have to 'watch' what you say.

To me, your heart and soul are linked into the values and principles you live by. These will be discussed in great detail in Chapter 10 – Leadership in the 21st Century.

Some people try to play games and are very calculated. They do things having worked out the cause and likely effects. Sometimes it works and sometimes it does not. Always the person who 'plays' like this will be caught out. However, the person who does things genuinely from the heart will show their principles and values in everything they do. It will shout out as loudly as if they were shouting through a megaphone.

CHAPTER 8

Motivation and Behaviour Shaping

What is all important

Motivation is a subject which has been written about forever. It is, however, key in your success. No matter what you do or where you are, you cannot do most things on your own, and therefore leading people and motivating them is critical.

Let's look at how. In our Advanced Power Listening we discussed letting the other person talk how to listen to them, and how to pause prior to replying. Well my next point is an extension of this. Quite frankly no one, except perhaps your mother and father, really care what you are! Or perhaps it is fairer to say others care about themselves more than they care about you. On the other hand you care about yourself and you know more about yourself and your experiences far better than anyone else. So when we put these groups together they want to talk about themselves and you want to talk about you! Oh! This really is not going to work unless one of you stops talking about yourself and listens to the other.

That should be you! Why? Well firstly, people think you are terribly interesting if you listen. I am not sure I can answer the question why they think this when *they* are doing the talking, but it works. Secondly, you can learn from their experiences. Those experiences can become your future 'hooks' into learning and understanding new things. So you must become genuinely interested in what someone else is saying. Don't pretend: it will show through. Become interested in other people and use that to create better relationships and build your Personal Knowledge Base.

Sigmund Freud said that everything you and I do springs from two motives: the sex urge and the desire to be great. Now whether that is true I do not know, but there is certainly an element in that we all want to live, have love and the feeling of importance and personal gratification. However, everyone is different.

People are not the same. Treat them differently

People are very different. If you treat them the same then you will not optimise your relationship. In motivation you need to understand what drives people, something we will return to in Chapter 10 – Leadership into the 21st Century.

There are different types of people and there are many ways to categorise people. Part of your success is to analyse people and understand what motivates them, what pushes their buttons, what drives them. It is then up to you to assist them in providing that motivation to achieve your joint objectives.

So I am going to categorise some types of people. My suggestion is that you make your own categories as this will ensure that you start to analyse people yourself.

The opposites

There are many different ways of thinking but I have come across a type of person who always sees things differently from me. In fact I can guarantee that when I think or say something they will think completely differently. If I say a glass is half-full, they will say it is half-empty, if I say something is white they will think it is black.

It is not easy to get on with someone who is always at odds with you but half of the battle is knowing who you are dealing with, and then you can converse with them to understand their position, instead of trying to work it through yourself.

The emotional

Overall men tend to be less emotional than women. This emotional line is a vast spectrum and some men can be more emotional than some women and so it is a sweeping statement. However, I have noted that these tendencies are there.

So adapt what you are doing to the different person. You would not try to sell an emotional person on pure logic; on the other hand you would not sell an unemotional person on pure emotion. Analyse the person and work out the best approach.

Open-minded and Closed-minded

Some people just will not keep an open mind or are not able to keep an open mind.

Within my working life I came across someone who always appeared to be totally closed-minded. There was a problem at work and they wrote a huge explanation from their point of view about what went wrong. I approached them to discuss it and they would not even accept that there might just be another view of the events. Their report was the only set of facts in the event. Obviously that was not true!

We all have different world views. Based on our experience and knowledge, our views will be not be the same as the next person. This continues to make it hard to see things from the other person's point of view. Closed-minded people will always need a more hands-on approach. You will need to show them with a physical representation. Let them discover how they may be wrong, preferably on their own.

Where they naturally fit

I am definitely a visual person; completely. The way to get something through to me is to draw a picture. Indeed I am lost without a whiteboard or flipchart when explaining something. What are you?

- Do you work by using your visual cortex?
- Do you use the sense of feel as the first base?
- Are you tactile and use your sense of touch?
- Do you use your sense of smell or your sense of hearing more?

People on average are:

- 65% visual

- 20% hearing
- 10% feeling

With the other senses split for the rest.

Knowing details about the person will help you with your approach.

Their use of vocabulary will give you a hint. Listen to the words then adjust your way of persuasion, communication and influence:

'I'll see you later'.
'That sounds good'.

You must try to get inside people and see the world from their perspective.

Motivation

How do we motivate. Firstly Maslow's Needs Theory has already been mentioned. It is worth buying his book and looking at the needs theory, if you are not aware of it. However, there are clearly a number of ways to motivate, depending on the individual and your analysis of them.

Let's look at some of the key factors in motivation:

- Fear
- Wealth
- Pleasure
- Pride and self-esteem

- The challenge
- Religion or passionate belief
- Praise
- Celebrate success

Incentives are based on individual drivers. The three most powerful motivators are fear, wealth and pleasure. However, they are also the three that can backfire the most.

Fear

Fear is a driver which I personally do not like. However, I would have to accept that for a short-term environment, fear is a hugely effective driver. People will go to great lengths in the name of fear. My concern is that life is not short-term. Drive people with fear and it will come back to haunt you in years to come. Fear has another side effect in that it continues to grow. The more fearful one is, the more one becomes, and if you are not careful it will consume you, it will paralyse you.

There is a very good book I would recommend you read to know more about working through and out of the other side of fear. *Feel the Fear and Do it Anyway* by Susan Jeffers or *How to Stop Worrying and Start Living* by Dale Carnegie. If you are using fear as a motivator use it wisely!

Wealth

Wealth is a driver and as an effective driver as fear. More people are motivated with the thought of wealth, gaining possessions, money and status. Lotteries generate a huge amount of money based on wealth as a motivator. Wealth is a little like fear in that it has some serious downsides. The more you seek wealth the more it can become greed and greed feeds itself to the point where you can never have enough. Yes a powerful motivator but again use it wisely!

Pleasure

The human condition is one that moves away from pain and towards pleasure. You may well have heard expressions such as 'the carrot and the stick', 'the carrot' being pleasure and 'the stick' being the pain.

Pain is a little like fear. It has some very negative downsides, unless used with care and sparingly, whilst pleasure is what most people seek.

Pride and self-esteem

Our pride and our self-esteem are very important to us. If you want to motivate someone, appeal to their pride and self-esteem.

When Aaron and Mali, my son and daughter, were 4 and 7 respectively, they would watch television. When the adverts came on they would always say 'Daddy, I want one of these toys on the television'. Firstly I said to them they needed to put it on their birthday list. Then we had a little game where I tried to suggest that everytime they saw an advert they needed to say 'No we don't want that'. Alas, the latter did not work but at least they put the ideas on their birthday list. They would suggest they wanted the items out of pleasure.

Most of the advertising we come across is based on fear, wealth creation, pleasure or appealing to pride and self-esteem. Look at adverts in the next few days and understand why they make you want to buy.

The challenge

Being challenged is another of the big motivators. Some people are not driven by fear or wealth and sometimes not even pride but they get their pleasure, their buzz, from the challenge. It can drive people to win the Olympic Games but it can also drive someone to do a fantastic job for you at work or get someone to join in with you at play.

Lay down the gauntlet and see the effect it has. Say to someone who is driven by challenge that they could not possibly achieve something and they will show you!

> When I ran my own manufacturing company I wanted someone to quickly check on something for me. I knew that she did not agree with me and thought it would be a waste of time and so I challenged her to prove she was right. In fact I bet her a Crunchie bar that she was wrong. In the end she proved I was wrong, however, I needed her to check it and so I achieved my objective by challenging her.

Religion or passionate belief

In history, religion has often been the cause of many wars. Do not underestimate it as a driver. Anyone driven by passionate belief or religion will usually be very motivated.

Praise

This follows a similar vein to 'thank you'. As humans we enjoy a 'pat on the back'. We enjoy being told that a good job has been done and yet we so rarely do it. In my career I have continuously promoted the action of telling people they have done a good job. We are all too quick to tell people when they have not performed.

If you look at children it is very clear to see they need encouragement and to be told that they have done well. The first time your son or daughter starts to do maths and gets the sums wrong, we don't scold them and say they are stupid, we encourage them by praising them for trying and moving on to help them so they can achieve the result.

We should do the same for adults. When they have done a good job, praise them and make sure others know they have done well. When they have not performed, privately and tactfully tell them and help them to improve.

Find a reason to praise someone for doing something today!

Celebrate success

There are many differences between England and America. One I have noticed is how we deal with success. People who are hugely and publicly successful in America are held up as heroes.

In England, more and more, they are held up to knock down. To me, this is a worrying trend but I remain convinced that one day this will change back. If we do not celebrate success and continue to knock down those who are successful then there is no incentive, no motivation to reach success.

Without the motivation and the incentive then success dies away and we no longer strive to achieve our real potential. So, at every opportunity, celebrate success, hold up people who have done well as heroes, and when you achieve something, find a way to carry out a positive celebration and a reward to those around you.

Behaviour shaping

Our own motivation is important, as is motivating others, however, being able to shape someone's behaviour on an ongoing basis has benefits far beyond motivation for now.

Being able to work with people to shape behaviour leads to enhanced motivation and allows any leader to get the most from their teams. After all, working with people is so important to achieving success.

What is behaviour shaping?

Behaviour is how we actually do things; our behaviour can be governed by many different things and learning to understand it is the subject of this section. The first thing is about controlling our own behaviour. Do you actually know how you will react in any given circumstance? Perhaps not, but unless it is an autonomic reaction you can have control over your reactions. Controlling your reactions is important in achieving success.

Have you ever noticed that in any given circumstance people react differently to things? It is the interpretation you give to what happens which is the first stage of governing your response. It is your own driving force, your own values which control your behaviour. If you can adapt your behaviour it will help in achieving success.

The first thing to work on then is how you shape your interpretation, which leads to your response. Personality patterns are primarily built up though your first 8 years of life. These form the basis of your behaviour to come. However, experience of life, different outcomes and the way you react can change the behaviour you have over time.

To change your behaviour you must be proactive rather than reactive and it must be about what you do rather than words. Knowing and understanding motivators can help with behaviour shaping but here we will take some of those ideas and add other behaviour shaping approaches.

Here are the top ten ways to shape behaviours:

- Use fear
- Praise desirable behaviour.
- Appeal and/or use values and principles
- Give choices
- Give rewards
- Use guilt

- Reinforce behaviour
- Use incompatible behaviour
- Put behaviour on cue
- Remove the benefit from the undesirable behaviour.

Use fear

We have already discussed fear as a motivator, but I would ask you not to use it as a primary behaviour shaping tool. There are many ways of shaping behaviour and there is already too much fear in this world. Watch, however, for when people try to manipulate you by using fear.

Praise desirable behaviour

Praise has also been discussed as a motivator and it is important that good behaviour, or behaviour you wish to promote, is praised. People respond to praise positively.

Appeal and/or use values and principles

Set down objectives and appeal for actions. Appeal to the values and principles that someone has. Firstly, of course, you need to understand the deep-set values and principles that the person lives by.

Give choices

Most people will take a lead and so if you channel someone's thinking by giving them two choices, most people, except stronger willed people, will find themselves taking one of those choices. You have directed and shaped their behaviour.

Leaders generate options and give choices in line with their needs. Good leaders go further and ensure that although a choice is given, without it being obvious, there is actually only one choice that makes any sense.

Give rewards

Rewards are absolutely critical in life. Give rewards to yourself but also to others. Rewards, as already described, move us towards pleasure. So when appropriate, reward yourself and others.

Use guilt

Guilt and shame are self-punishment. The human condition has considerable ability to use this to destroy itself. I have seen it used so often, causing severe pain to people. I add it in here because you must know when people are using it against you, but I would ask you never to use it on someone. Life is just too short to make people so unhappy.

Reinforce behaviour

Reinforcing behaviour that has been seen is a major way in cementing the behaviour and getting the behaviour repeated. Reinforcement can be internalised or externalised. Internal re inforcement is far, far more powerful than reinforcement from outside. For instance: 'I feel good if I do this' is internal reinforcement.

Reinforcing behaviour is always best done at the time or just after the time of the behaviour. If it happens during the behaviour the maximum reinforcement will be gained.

To stop a behaviour stop the reinforcement and if it has no internal reinforcement it will extinguish itself.

Punishment is a negative reinforcement. However, punishment not only has an effect on the person punished but also the person punishing. Ironically, punishment can induce a certain pleasure. This is something to be aware of: adjust your behaviour accordingly.

Punishment can be a deterrent, as long as the stakes are high enough and the probability high enough to get caught.

> *I used to look after a small fleet of vehicles which had tachographs in the lorries. The chances of getting caught were slight when I first joined the company as they were not being checked. I instituted our legal requirement to check at random. However, it was still a very small probability that an infringement would be caught and if they did, the punishment would be disciplinary action and perhaps dismissal. People still broke the rules because the probability was slight.*

If the punishment was continuous i.e. as you exhibited the behaviour, then it would effectively change your behaviour very rapidly.

To me, positive ways of changing behaviours are better.

Use incompatible behaviour

Behaviour can be altered by instructing someone to carry out incompatible behaviour, i.e. if you give them something to eat they cannot eat and smoke. The behaviour of smoking will be reduced.

If you feel lonely you switch on the television and it stops you being lonely. It is an incompatible behaviour.

Put behaviour on cue

Putting the behaviour on cue is manipulative but it can stop the behaviour destroying situations.

Schools use this to control children, especially when you have a considerable number all making a noise. In my son and daughter's school, if the teacher holds up their index finger everyone has to be quiet. I've seen it work.

Remove the benefit from the undesirable behaviour

If you are driving in a 30 mile per hour zone but people are aware that a rolling roadblock is ahead travelling at 30 miles per hour then there is no benefit with speeding, and most people will not speed.

Remember you CANNOT reinforce behaviour which does not occur which is why it must be reinforced at the time it actually happens.

Key messages

To understand how to change someone's behaviour you need to understand them.

Taking an example: are there really, really bad people out there?

If you ask them, they would probably say 'No'. Everyone has a different world view and different perspective on life based upon their knowledge and experience.

It is important to understand their perspective because it gives us the starting point to change behaviour.

When was the last time you did something that somebody thought was wrong or naughty? Did you know? If you go down a one-way street the wrong way because you did not see the sign, are you a bad person? Have you done wrong?

When was the last time you criticised yourself? If you do not believe that you have done anything wrong then why should others believe that they have done things wrong? This is why values and principles are so important! We take our rights and wrongs from our values and principles which are mostly established before the age of 8.

> *How many times have you seen someone driving along with their fog lights blazing at you or driving in the middle lane when the driving lane is free on 'their' side of the motorway? Some just do not care but some do. Some just do not know they are doing anything wrong.*
>
> *So we have two sets of people here:*

- *Those that do know they are doing wrong and don't care (a few)*
- *Those that do not know they are doing wrong (the majority)*

Therefore when someone does something wrong what use does scolding them achieve? I accept at times punishment is needed but punishment will not change behaviour if the behaviour is not deemed to be flawed. So remember criticism is futile and puts the person 'on the defensive'.

Do it or not

There are very few reasons why people do not do things when they have agreed to do them. I worked with many voluntary groups in my twenties and thirties and the one thing that amazed me was that people did not do something after they said they would. I began to ask 'Why?' And the more I asked, the more the answers came to me. I wrote them down.

People do not do things they have agreed to because

- They do not have enough time (low priority)
- They cannot do it
- They don't know how to start to do it
- They really don't want to do it
- They don't really understand it needs to be done
- They don't really appreciate it is up to them to do it
- They don't think it is worth doing anyway

For each of these different reasons there is a different way of approaching them.

If someone says they do not have enough time, then I would say 'Join the club, nor do I'. It is not, however, about time but the priority placed on it. If something is not a priority for someone from their point of view and it is from yours, sell it to them!

If they cannot do it then get someone else to, or better still show them how to do it so that they can next time.

In most situations I have found that people tend to know how to do it. However, they have no confidence to start it and have trouble with this starting point. In which case help them with starting it and then withdraw and let them complete it.

If they don't want to do it, you need to persuade them. Use your influence!

Sometimes, even though they may have agreed to do it, they still do not understand it needs to be done. They need to be convinced. Sell the importance of it and how big that will make them feel.

They may still not appreciate that it is up to them to do it. They may be expecting someone else to start it. Help put them straight and get it started.

Finally, they may be holding out on the grounds that they don't think it is worth doing anyway! Over to you and your persuasive skills.

CHAPTER 9

Networking

Most people have heard the saying 'it is not *what* you know but *who* you know'. For me the reality is both. You need to have experience and you need to have knowledge, and when that experience and knowledge come together, with opportunities presented by the relationships you have, then usually it leads to successful paths. It is true that sometimes you do not need to know anything and that you can get where you want simply through the people you know but it is often short-lived and ends up being unpleasant. To me it is like perception. Perception is king, but reality rules, something we will discuss later. In any case, reality will always 'catch you' in the end.

Networking means you need to put yourself at the heart of other people's lives. It means getting on with them, and it means being genuinely interested in them.

Over the years I have kept in touch with many of my friends from school, college, university and work. When I looked recently, I had a database of 415 people. I am not expecting these people to help me out or to make me successful, I just like to keep in touch when I can. These days there are websites such as Friends Reunited or professional sites such as LinkedIn to help you keep in touch.

I read a report which said that a survey in the early 2000s showed that out of 100 chief executive officers 70%, if presented with two identical candidates, were more likely to give jobs to people who they knew or who went to the same school as themselves.

Networking is sometimes looked upon as 'evil'. There are even organisations set up which help with networking, such as the Masons. However you do networking, it is a very important part of your progression to success.

How to network effectively

Firstly, without any doubt, you have to be proactive and do things. You have to join organisations and get out. Staying in watching TV just will not do it. Are you a member of any groups in the evening? Do you go to meetings of like-minded people?

Join organisations

It is fine to join organisations but I suggest that you actually get really involved in those organisations. That is where you make the friends and can really network.

> *In my youth I was in a choir, I joined a political organisation and I joined a theatre group. I became a school governor at the age of 23 and that was just the start. I got out and about.*

Work with people

Do things for people and expect NO return. If you expect a return it becomes a business proposition and you will only get your 'pound of flesh'.

Ensure at events contact is made and secured over time

Drop a note in or follow up with a note to anyone, at any time. If they do something for you or even if you see them in the street and have not seen them for a while a 'great to see you' note says a lot. Get some note cards and make sure it is handwritten if at all possible.

Professional bodies

Professional bodies are an excellent way to mix with people with the same interests and often the same career paths and jobs. They have magazines which you can write to and they usually meet regularly. Go along to the meetings and become a part of the group. Don't sit at the back but talk to people; after all, you all have something in common.

> *I am a member of the Institute of Lighting Engineers, a member of the Chartered Management Institute, a fellow of the Chartered Institute of Personnel and Development, and Institute of Directors to name but a few. In the past I have been involved in other groups such as the Institute of Electrical Engineers.*
>
> *I have been on the committee in both the Chartered*

Institute of Personnel and Development and the Institute of Directors.

**Remember everyone you meet can form
a better part of an expanding network**

When you are meeting with those people remember how to get on with them:

- Remember that they have an opinion and you need to respect it
- Remember not to criticise and say they are wrong
- Remember to listen and not talk
- Learn to understand them more

CHAPTER 10

Power Perception and Intuition

The first thing I am to write here is 'Perception is king but reality rules'.

This chapter will show you just how powerful perception is for both you and others. Learn to understand perception otherwise it may well be your undoing. Intuition is also important, learn to read it.

Many people have said that if you do the right thing then it will 'all turn out right in the end'. I agree partly. You should always do what is right and that will come from your values and principles. However, you must also work on perception because if this is wrong it can bring you down and close doors.

*In 2008 my sister briefly moved into the area where I was living. Some people at my daughter's school saw me giving her a kiss and a hug and (shock, horror!) over a few weeks I did it several times. My wife was not anywhere to be seen at the time and I assure you: the tongues were wagging, until on one occasion when I introduced one of them to **my sister**. The horror on this individual's face made me realise what they had been thinking: I had been cheating on my wife. Not at all true but that was their perception.*

There are many examples I could cite but my advice is to be aware of the perception of others if you can.

For many years I taught politicians and their whole career was, and continues to be, built on perception. As long as people perceive they are doing a good job then they will be elected back into power every four or five years. The only thing is, if you are doing a bad job, it will catch you in the end.

We are all guilty of falling prey to perception. You meet someone in the street with multicoloured hair and depending upon your world view, you categorise them.

> I have dealt with human resources for a few companies and so I have had a good number of people coming to my office for job interviews. In the early 2000s someone who could only be considered 'a lout' came in. He had earrings, tattoos and walked in with a swagger. Well I nearly threw him out there and then. However, I have a strict way of interviewing and I thought 'No, I will stick to my process'. Well when he opened his mouth, my initial perception changed completely. He was an honest, sincere person and went on to be one of my star employees, a real high flyer.

Perception is often flawed, but:

Perception is king even if reality rules

Your perception

The perception you give is vital to your success.

The person, who enthusiastically bounds up to you smiling and gives you a firm handshake, leaves you with a strong positive perception. The person who has a limp handshake tells you something else. How do you greet people?

The fundamental core here is 'reality is not always good enough'. The perception of the reality is as important as the reality.

Not everyone will like you or want to be your friend and nor should they. However, you need to be aware of how you are perceived and decide whether that is a true reflection of you. If it is a true reflection then good. If it is not then you have to ensure that the perception you give off is as close to reality as you can get it. If your reality is in order then you will be fine.

This reality is vital when it relates to your boss. Many people think you should 'manage your boss'. I disagree, but would accept you should manage the perception they may have if it is at odds with the truth.

Communication becomes very important in perception, and how you phrase things is especially important. For instance, saying that 'this year we have increased our turnover by £50,000' sounds good, doesn't it? If I said 'we have doubled our turnover in just 1 year', which sounds better?

So when you have good results or successes to promote, it is important to draw attention to those results in a, 'non-boasting' manner. Perhaps a monthly report updating the boss on the current situation.

When I was a young teenager I fancied a girl and I plucked up the courage to go up and ask her out. Literally the time was there and I was ready but in a conversation with another girl she called this girl 'a moose' just before I asked her out. Well far from being nice, it had an effect on me and I did not ask her out. This bothered me for weeks until I realised that my perception of her had changed.

So with perception, ensure that not only reality exists and is good but that everyone perceives the reality.

Do not fall down the trap of politicians where they try to make people perceive something different to reality.

Remember:

Perception is king, but reality rules.

CHAPTER 11

Leading the Way
& Getting Your Own Way

Advanced Power Negotiation

It took me a long time to realise but if you want your own way
then you need to negotiate. You need to get others to agree to
your way of thinking. As my children were growing up, they
were absolutely brilliant at negotiating with me, my wife and
even each other. Oh, how I learned from them!

This section will discuss the various techniques there are to
identify and negotiate deals from small to major mediation
tasks.

However, negotiation is not something that is learned. It will
only become real by doing it. If you feel shy or uncomfortable at
this point, I totally understand but you can get over it. We have
been bartering and negotiating since there were beings on this
earth. Don't let some 'conditioning' remove that special ability.
You remember the one we all had as children?

> *'Mummy, if I am a good boy can I have a sweet after
> dinner?' How could you possibly say no? However, he
> is just selling something that should happen anyway.*

*He should be a good boy and we all get suckered in by
it, including me, every time.*

Negotiation is an art and I want you to promise yourself that
you will go out tomorrow and find an opportunity to use one of
the tips and techniques in this section. Promise? If you really do
promise then I will let you read on...

The more you negotiate, the more you will grow in confidence
about doing it. You will get what you want and the other party
will get what they want. How could you fail to want to be a part
of this? You will save money and, trust me, eventually you will
enjoy the process.

You will feel the power that comes from a successful
negotiation.

Imagine if on every deal you do, you get something more than
you expect. It all adds up. In the meantime, as well as getting
what you want, you make a lifelong friend. Those are the sorts
of results that negotiation brings.

There are very clear and easy to understand rules which can be
applied to negotiation and there are easy to implement
techniques to be learned.

Advanced Power Negotiation is a process by which all parties
move from diverse to mutually beneficial positions by means of
discussions.

A subtle mix of:

•   Diplomacy

- Persuasion
- Compromise
- Advanced Power Communication
  a) Effective Speaking
  b) Effective Voice Control
  c) Body Language
- Advanced Power Listening

leads to the art of negotiation.

> *I attended a convention some time ago and I wanted to purchase some session tapes. Now they were offering a deal: buy two tapes, get another for £10 and a free tee shirt. This was quite good value since the tapes were £19 each. I thought that it was a great opportunity to try my new-found skill.*
>
> *'Now I'll have the three tapes and if you let me have another tape for a tenner, you can add one tape to the sale" I said. As this was on top of the first offer, it was two tapes for a tenner and so this was a 'win-win' scenario.*
>
> *Well I felt a little bad about asking this but the chap came back immediately and said. 'I'll tell you what I'll do: I will let you have the £10 off and two free tee shirts if you buy the other tape.' Needless to say, I bought it. He was happy and so was I. The tee shirts were worth £5 each.*
>
> *No one felt uncomfortable in the end.*

At that point I decided I would like to try this negotiation over and over. Negotiation, however, is not only for buying goods. When you want someone to do something for you it is negotiation or persuasion. How many times have you said to a friend, look if you can do this for me then I will do that for you.

Get over the feeling that you are making a fool of yourself. You are not!

What is negotiation?

We negotiate much of the time without realising it. Therefore it is silly that when we come to really 'negotiate' we feel difficult about it.

The main rule, for me, behind a successful negotiation, is it must always be a 'win-win' situation.

If there is no 'win-win' then it is not a negotiation, perhaps a dictatorship but not a negotiation.

Whenever we negotiate our objective is to:

- Get what we want
- Get for the other parties what they want.

The strongest position in negotiation is the position where you can walk away easily. If you can do that you have all of the aces.

So how do we do Advanced Power Negotiation?

Let me first reintroduce V.A.P.E.R.:

- Vision
- Analysis
- Planning
- Execution
- Review

As explained earlier, this process is fundamental for management and can be applied for negotiation.

Vision:
- What is it you want?

Analysis:
- What is it that they want?
- Where are they coming from?
- What are their strengths and weaknesses?
- Where are you coming from?
- What are your strengths and weaknesses?

Planning:
- Plan your strategy in the negotiation.
- Are you willing to give in and at what point?
- Can you give them anything that costs you nothing yet is in line with their objectives?

Execution:
- Actually carry out the negotiation.
- Always leave it and come back if you want more time. You never have to complete at that moment despite what the other person says.

Review:
- Always review and ensure your and their objectives are met. If not learn from the review.

Vision

First of all you must have your vision, target, purpose or goal. Without this you are not ready to even start a negotiation. You need to write down clearly what you are trying to achieve by this negotiation and then you must see yourself in your own mind achieving the result you wrote down.

Analysis

* What does the other person want?
* What motivates them?
* What will they be happy with?
* What pressures are there on them to come away with what?
* What is their bottom line?
* What might they walk away from the table with?

The list goes on!

It is surprisingly easy to satisfy all demands.

Analysis is also the time that you bring forward your 'intelligence'. This may be from research or just your knowledge of the situation but this should form part of the analysis. Take an example: if you were doing a negotiation and you knew the other person had been told that they would be fired if they did not successfully negotiate the contract, how powerful would your position be in the negotiation?

Read their body language. What does it say? Body language is something we will cover in more detail later.

Planning

Strategy is important in negotiation. As with anything else:

- Plan your strategy.
- Is it going to be an offensive one or a defensive one?

If a car dealer asks what price you are looking for and you say '£6,000', then if that is ridiculous, he will have the upper hand. If it is too high he will again have the upper hand.

So, to the plan:

- Make sure your plan is thorough.
- Fact find by whatever means and use your analysis of the opposition in the negotiation to think about tactics.
- Work out how to smoke out and confirm their own concession list. What are they willing to give away?

If you were going to buy a car, you would need to look on the Internet or Parkers car price guide to plan and consider. Why not research for any negotiation?

Rehearsal allows you to identify weaker parts of your argument. If it is an important negotiation then rehearse with a friend or colleague, if you can.

In any negotiation, don't move on with an issue until it has been sorted. Never say that you will come back to that point, unless it is a part of your strategy to deal with it later on. It will become an objection that cannot be resolved and that breaks the negotiation.

Consider in your plan the techniques that would be most

effective when negotiating with this person or persons. This can be defined from the analysis made at the beginning.

Remember the long-term relationship vs short-term gain.

In your tactics, consider your own strengths. Plan to use them in the negotiation.

- Set your sub-goals.
- Define your minimum/maximum position and list the options and expectations.
- Drive through those expectations and for heaven's sake do not let anyone else get a sight of your plan!

Execution

Negotiating power:

- The negotiation is with you, use you and everything you are, to be better at negotiating.
- Use your experience and techniques in negotiating.
- Communicate effectively using your words and body language to achieve the result you want.
- Use the Knowledge Power from your own Personal Knowledge Base.
- Keep in control.
- Stay alert with a high level of energy and enthusiasm.
- Remember Advanced Power Listening; listen and talk less.
- Remember to use questions wisely.
- Get some agreement and some commitment along the way at each stage of the negotiation.

- Use any larger group or organisation power.
- Take risks – no risk, no gain!
- Remember it will be hard work, commit to it and stick with it until it is done.
- Remember the 'win-win' scenario.
- Prepare, prepare, prepare.
- Do not assume anything in a negotiation.

Review

A famous quote I once heard 'If you make a mistake once and do not learn from it, you are destined to make it again and again and again'.

The V.A.P.E.R. steps are ALL vital. Miss any out and you will be in trouble. You will not be a successful negotiator.

Go back and review where it went right and where it could be improved.

Techniques in Negotiation

Give and get

You should always get something when you give something in a negotiation. Never give anything away for nothing. If someone asks for a concession get something back for it.

'OK if we reduce the working time by half an hour the staff must all wear bow ties'. OK that maybe a silly suggestion but the give and get does NOT have to be related.

Example:

> 'Well I could only lower the price to that level if you were to buy 500'.

Remember all parties must feel like they have won. They have to come away with what they wanted.

Nibble

You may have seen 'Columbo' a popular seventies TV programme. He has an interview with a suspect and goes to leave. At that point, usually just by the door, when the suspect has relaxed, he always turns to them and asks them the hitting question of the enquiry. The 'nibble' is that little bit more you gain when everyone thinks the contract is signed and sealed and all that is needed is the delivery.

> *My wife and I were in Cyprus a while back and I saw a lovely chess set. Upon checking with other establishments the price seemed quite good and so we attempted to do some negotiating.*
>
> *It was interesting but he was a good negotiator using many of the techniques we have already covered. He also used the 'nibble'. At the very end I was ready to purchase he said 'Oh that is the price is for cash' knowing that the credit card costs the seller between 1.5 and 4%. That is the nibble. I was committed by that stage.*
>
> *He nibbled away my advantage at the last minute.*
>
> *He said we could have a discount for not having a box, showing a level of taking something for giving something.*

Eventually we reduced the price by only £4 but with the box thrown in.

Silence
People find silence uncomfortable so keeping silent often means the other person will take that as a negative reaction and will come back with a better position.

The advantage
Do you have something on the person or organisation you are negotiating with? Something you know that gives you the upper hand, something you can slip into the negotiation or hint at the successful outcome helping?

Responsive actions
Put in some tactics of your own.

Respond to others negotiating tactics, which can only be done if you know the techniques well and can spot them. If you are expecting particular tactics or you know a person uses a particular type then plan to counter them.

Bait and switch
Go off in one direction talking about something or negotiating a particular point and then change at the last minute to something more sensitive. 'So are you in agreement that you like the blue Widget and would like to buy it for £70?' Once they have your commitment then they say, 'Oh sorry we have run out of the blue ones and so I'll give you the yellow instead'.

My reply to that would be: 'Fine, let's knock off £10 for the yellow.'

The famous intake of breath

Whatever you do, whatever the price, always give those you are negotiating with a sharp intake of breath when they give you a price or a condition. The other party will always respond and you will be surprised at their response sometimes.

The Sales trial balloon

'So if I was to lower the price by £2 you would buy £30,000 worth?' It is a trial to see what level you will go to without actually making an offer or putting down any concessions. They are trying to flush you out.

The trial balloon also helps to overcome objections. If that is not the main objection they will tell you it now.

Coercion

Convince someone around to your view; influence them to agree with you. Show them that what you want will also benefit them.

Commitment questioning

Gain some commitment along the way. 'So you definitely want white?'

Red herring

You make the other party feel that something is very important to you and then give in, ensuring that you achieve what is really important for you. 'OK but if I give in on this important factor then at least give me this to show for it'.

Blocking

You have the power and the ability to block others from satisfying their interest.

Use it carefully and tactfully. If not, you could end up with enemies and not a 'win-win' situation.

Bad behaviour
There is no need to either use or put up with bad or aggressive behaviour. It is not to be entertained at all in Advanced Power Negotiation. You should, however, recognise it when it is being applied to you.

Compromise
When you get to compromise in the negotiation then it has really broken down as it will not be a 'win-win' situation.

Walk Away
The ability to leave a negotiation gives you the upper hand. You have a considerable advantage if you can walk away from a negotiation. Obviously you are weakened if you *have* to strike a deal.

Styles of negotiation:
- Competitive — get most for yourself
- Accommodative — give most to the other
- Avoiding — steer clear of negative
- Compromising — Style split difference
- Collaborative — most for both parties

Negotiation 'no-nos'
- Stuff the other party
- Get tied up on one subject

People often fall into the trap of negotiating one thing at a time. Do not do this. Trade things off with each other. Negotiate as a whole picture. Do not bargain down to one obstacle. You will not reach the 'win-win' scenario.

Often salesmen will do this. 'Right that's everything except the price' and they never make the sale. I have seen this happen with my own sales force.

No *negatives*
Being negative in anything does not work but in negotiation and selling it produces winners and losers. Do not let this happen. Stay positive and focussed so that all parties can win and neither you nor the other party lose. All needs can be met if handled positively.

Compromise is a last resort and really the negotiation has not been successful.

Remember the following tips:

- Keep an eye on the big picture and the plan.
- Keep control at all times.
- Keep your personal power firm, energetic, but always polite.
- Overcome objections from the other parties.
- Put people under pressure by telling them time is running out.
- Use the scarcity card if at all possible. I only have one left.
- Be patient yourself as it wears the opposition down.
- Take it or leave it. Remember the power if you can walk away.
- Give in, in a planned manner designed still to achieve above your minimum position.
- Budget excuse is always a good one.
- Using statistics – highs, lows – averages.
- 'Good guy, bad guy' routine.
- Reaching the bottom line.

Deadlocks

When in a deadlock, consider the following approaches: (Always take time out if needed.)

- Mediation.
- Time to think.
- Prepare to walk away.
- Review tactics.
- Move on if you must.
- Move back to pitfalls and give in something, but get something in return.
- DO NOT Compromise. This generally becomes a 'lose-lose' situation.

Always review your negotiation afterwards! How could it have been more effective?

Advanced Power Negotiation can save time, money, stress, relationships, oppositions and reputations. It can also enhance and build long-term relationships.

When negotiating, it is worth understanding the different types of people you are working with. Here are some examples:

Different types of negotiators

There is the aggressive negotiator; they go for the total win.

They often look for one-sided gains and can use negative behaviour such as threats and insults. They will often withhold information and stretch the facts.

Diplomat

This is the type of person who will try to talk you out of something, or into it.

They tend to go for agreements and cultivate a relationship. They will also generally act in a fair, polite and courteous manner. They share information and will often make unilateral concessions.

The reluctant negotiator

This type of person will not really want to negotiate. This is a distraction.

They do not want to lose and have survival as their main aim. They tend to dither, delay and stall and are very non committal.

The idealist

The truth seeker is often in a world of their own. They go for truth and justice above the nitty gritty of the negotiation. They are honest and sincere but they are usually inflexible and quite intense.

The analyst

An analyst wants to sift through and understand. Part of the negotiation for them is to build knowledge. Be careful, they can keep you at the table for hours.

They are often thoughtful and have objective criteria. They seek multiple options.

My brother and I were buying a television. This TV was expensive and £4,500 was eventually spent in the shop. We negotiated a DVD machine plus some gold plated scart leads and a few DVD disks. It might not sound much but when you consider we would not have even had that unless we overcame the embarrassment of asking:

'Well that's a considerable amount of money, how about throwing in a DVD player?' then once the transaction was almost over 'oh we need leads. I'm sure you're not going to quibble about that! Are you?'

Notice the nibble technique here. You are almost making them feel that if they say 'Yes' they are being petty.

And from the female in our group 'Perhaps we could have a DVD to test the system?' These techniques worked.

Remember: keep it simple stupid, the KISS principle.

Don't put down markers such as price and delivery too early.

Negotiation is about seeking settlement as near to the other parties' bottom line whilst maximising your own interests.

Mediation

I am covering mediation at the same time as negotiation as there are some similarities. There will be times in the Advanced Power State when you need to be able to mediate.

It is a very important tool in your toolbox. There are, however, times to use it and times not to use it.

Mediation is there to diffuse natural conflict.

In mediation, even more than in negotiation, it is vitally important to find out the style of negotiation being used, and work out why there is conflict in that style. It may be that one party cannot get on with that style. This is done at the analysis stage or at the first review.

Mediation process

Take the fixed positions and put those positions clearly to all groups. Then:

- Let groups retire to a private place to discuss what has been put to them.
- This should always be in separate areas, preferably separate rooms.

The mediator will always shuffle between the rooms and the groups. The mediator will:

- Make offers
- Try 'What if' scenarios
- Clarify points
- Add information
- Suggest ways forward
- Add encouragement

The mediator must be careful not to gain ownership of the challenges and therefore continue to maintain the trust of all sides. They must be independent and have no interest in any part of what is going on.

If it is perceived the mediator is not totally neutral, mediation will not work, and so you must change the mediator.

All parties must agree to the mediator and to mediation.

The mediator must be trusted by all sides and must be objective.

Set out and agree the plan for the mediation and give a deadline. If the mediation is not over by the deadline, close it and move on.

If it is then the decision of all afterwards to return to the table, then you may do so.

Consider the use of binding arbitration.

As with negotiation, follow the V.A.P.E.R. trail!

CHAPTER 12

Advanced Power Communications and Presentations

In my view, communication is one of the poorest practised skills of the current day. People often do not know how to communicate effectively and it causes no end of problems.

This section will go through tips and techniques for improving your communications and presentations. You will only reach the Advanced Power State if you can present and communicate well.

Earlier in this book we said that almost everything you do is by interacting with someone else. Communication is, of course, the method you use to interact with them.

Introduction to Communication

Understanding how people communicate effectively will allow you to grow enormously as a person. It is through communication that your vision can be realized, your instructions can be carried out and your influence can grow.

With communication your own words and actions can positively work for you or against you. Communication, as already stated, is not just words. It can be by facial expression, body language or even tone of voice and atmosphere given off subconsciously.

Communication uses total cortical and sensory skills. When we communicate with people, we need to do it on a basis that they understand. Effective communication is two-way!

Different types of people have different, optimum ways of being communicated with and although most are visual, some are aural and some through touch. Which do you use?

If someone says 'I see you have two of those' they are visual people. 'I hear…', listening people, 'I understand…', analytical people.

As with all brain activity, when communicating, the brain works by associations. So when communicating verbally, start the communication with opening the folder, like you would on a computer. If you are to talk about your wedding then the first words would contain 'my wedding'. The file in the other party's head is then open and associations can start to take place.

For example: 'My wedding … is the best that I can afford'.

As opposed to:

'I am going to have the best …wedding I can afford'.

People will be able to process the information better, faster, and retain it for longer if you open the folder first. Whereas starting without the subject in place gives less time for the visualisation process to work.

An example would be a speaker saying:

> 'To allow this planning permission, though, we must do the following:
>
> 1...
> 2...
> 3...'

The same applies when you are communicating in a presentation or a speech. You need to be able to;

- Stand up with confidence and present your ideas
- Communicate those ideas effectively
- Persuade the audience to your point of view
- Plan and organise an efficient seminar
- Use presentation equipment effectively

Firstly define the reason for your presentation. Remember: V.A.P.E.R.

- Is it to 'sell' an item or an idea?
- Is it to inform a group?
- Is it to convince someone to take action in a certain way?
- Is it to communicate ideas for a particular reason?

It is only with the objective defined that you can hope to make it a success.

Body Language

Body language is a subject all on its own. Get yourself a good book. For now here is a taster:

It is not only verbal language that is vital but body language. Body language accounts for over 50% of your communication.

For instance:

Throughout history the open palm has been taken to symbolise truth, honesty, allegiance and submission. In court the tradition of taking the bible in one hand and holding the other up, palm open, often still stands.

A palm upwards is also a beggar action and a palm downwards is constraint e.g. shaking hands.

Finger pointing is often seen as an aggressive action.

Body language also comes into presentations. For instance, you will find many speakers speak from behind a table. I generally don't. The reason is that the table is protection for the speaker and a barrier for the others.

If I walk towards you or lean towards you, I am bringing you into the session, and you feel like you are taking part.

Some other examples of the importance of body language are:

• Drumming fingers along the table shows boredom
• Open arms are inviting, welcoming
• Closed arms are protecting but also providing a barrier
• A smile is also inviting, welcoming and accepting. It is international

Watch your:

- Open posture
- Forward lean
- Touch
- Eye contact
- Nodding

The human face sends out a considerable amount of verbal and non-verbal communications. A leader, a manager or just a friend needs to use the communication as effectively as possible.

Remember: to get on with people you must communicate!

That is an incredibly quick taster to body language. It is a fascinating subject. Find a book as it is well worth it.

Preparation for your presentation

Preparation and goal setting are the two most important philosophies in life let alone in just presentations. Here are some tips for presenting effectively, although much of the information now given for presentations are just as valid in talking to a group of two people as a group of 100. Go through and decide the salient points depending upon your audience make-up and size.

Prepare yourself a pack which contains everything you will need for your presentation. This can be done for whatever the type of presentation you may be engaged in. If you think it is a considerable amount of work, you're right. But the next time you go to give a similar presentation it will save you starting from scratch. It will save you hours. A pre-prepared pack will also give you added confidence.

Presenter's Pack

The presenter's pack consists of:

- A sketch of the session with guidance and information (not a script)
- Model copies of handouts for distribution:
  a) before
  b) during
  c) after
- A file and computer for presenting the Powerpoint slides, or acetates for overhead projectors, if appropriate.
- A final checklist of things to do before the seminar.

Presenter's responsibilities

The organising presenter's responsibilities are to:

1. Contact the customer and talk through requirements
2. Liaise over rooms
3. Arrange for suitable layout
4. Request coffee and tea for trainers and participants
5. Send master copies of handouts to be photocopied
6. Note the number of handout copies required
7. Note the colour of paper for each handout to be printed on
8. Note for the distribution of handouts, in advance or not
9. Arrange:
   a) Flip chart
   b) Markers
   c) OHP
   d) Other Equipment
10. Liaise with any co-presenters and co-ordinators about roles.

Tips on training presentations

'Whenever people are involved nothing is straightforward'.

As with all presentations, use V.A.P.E.R, objective, purpose or vision followed by the training needs analysis. Plan what you need to cover, deliver it, and review it, to ensure it achieves the vision or the objective. Remember V.A.P.E.R.

Effective training requires the trainer to:

* Generate an effective environment
* Impart information
* Motivate and listen
* Receive and evaluate feedback

To have two-way communications, the trainer must know the audience. This is a part of the analysis stage:

* Who are they?
* What do they already know?
* How much can they absorb?
* What they are trying to achieve?

A trainer or presenter needs to:

* Create a level of credibility with the audience before or at the start of the seminar. However, before is always better
* Get their attention within 45 seconds or the message will be harder to deliver
* Build a rapid rapport – from the initial greeting and throughout the presentation

- Rapidly support or build a foundation of knowledge at base level, something often missed by very professional presenters
- Reinforce basic ideas constantly

Subject matter

To run an effective seminar or presentation the trainer/speaker must know the subject matter.

It is important to know:

- Where to find information?
- How to use it?
- What material to use?

To define the subject and make the seminar relevant requires:

- The title to be related to the subject
- What is essential and useful to be sorted and used?
- The 'shape' of the talk to be decided, with a distinct beginning, middle and end planned
- Good timing
- Suitable visual aids and physical samples, if possible, should be used

Remember: thorough preparation will give you added confidence.

When undertaking a seminar or presentation:

- Know your purpose

- Appreciate what you are trying to achieve
- Decide upon communication or instruction
- Define the objectives of your talk
- Know the reason for your talk
- Know the reason for you giving the talk

Two further tips

Send biographical details in advance: it allows the seminar members to become more familiar with you.

If possible, get notes on those attending to familiarise yourself with your own audience.

Some Tips and Techniques

Over the years I have come across many techniques which will help in delivering seminars or presentations. I have listed the most important ideas here. Use these ideas and tips for you future presentations and seminars

- Prepare and plan your presentation or seminar
- Use clear short sentences and limit details
- Repeat points up to three times for longer retention
- Use little stories and anecdotes
- Know your facts
- Make eye contact as naturally but as often as possible
- Understand and know your audience
- Energise yourself
- Smile, smile, smile. Be inviting
- Keep your talking slot to 20 minutes

- Dress smartly and comfortably
- Dramatise those ideas. People get emotionally involved in drama

Prepare and plan your presentation or seminar
In all the time I have been teaching presentations and giving presentations or seminars, a key point that continues to be important, is the preparation and the planning. The more you put into the preparation the more you will feel comfortable with the delivery and thus the more effective you will be. Preparation and planning also means practise delivering your work.

Use clear short sentences and limit details
It always amazes me that people use long sentences and long words. People should always communicate in a language and a way that is simple and easy to understand.

Repeat points up to three times for longer retention
Repetition is globally recognised as one of the main ways to improve retention of information. So the important points should be repeated a number of times during the presentation or seminar.

Use little stories and anecdotes
Little stories and anecdotes make the presentation or seminar more interesting. People remember stories, analogies, anecdotes and examples far more than theory. However, do not overdo it.

Know your facts
There is nothing more important in presenting than knowing your subject. Research it beforehand!

Make eye contact as naturally but as often as possible
People want you to talk to them and so it is important to make

eye contact with as many people in the audience as frequently as you can.

Understand and know your audience
If you understand or know your audience, you will find it easier to understand what angle or view they might have of the presentation. You can then plan and deliver the presentation in a more effective way for those people, perhaps giving them more relevant examples.

Energise yourself
In any presentation, there is a real need for energy. If the presenter lacks energy then the whole presentation has a great risk of being drab and something that the audience will not listen to effectively and thus will not achieve the presenter's objectives.

Smile, smile, smile. Be inviting
People are more receptive to inviting people. If you smile, people are immediately disposed to listen to you and take in what you are saying.

Keep your talking slot to 20 minutes
It is generally accepted in delivering seminars and presentations that people start to lose their concentration after 20 minutes of someone talking. There are ways to extend this attention time, such as using several presenters and interactive elements.

Dress smartly, and comfortably
When you dress smartly, generally you feel better and more confident in your delivery. Try it! The only caveat is that it is wise to dress for your audience. It would be pointless you being in a suit when everyone in the room is in a leather jacket!

Dramatise those ideas

People get emotionally involved in drama. Not only do people tend to enjoy it more but they will also remember it more.

Those techniques will help you in the delivery of successful seminars and presentations. It is also worth noting that the beginning and the end of any presentation are critical to its success. We have already mentioned attracting attention within 45 seconds, so start with something which creates an impact:

- Say something surprising, startling, shocking (but also relevant)
- Ask a question
- Tell a story
- Tell a joke (take great care as some jokes can backfire)

Do something that will attract the attention of your audience. Often the only way of knowing what will, is by talking to them before the session, and finding out about your audience before getting there.

Another useful tip is to avoid apologising in a presentation or seminar. My general rule is: do not apologise in this forum unless there is a clear need to.

Going back to basics then: V.A.P.E.R.

Vision:
- Clearly define your vision
- Clearly draw the vision
- Clearly list the goals to reach your vision
- Highlight how this seminar will help in the goals

Analysis:
- Gather yourself
- Gather materials
- Where are you now?
- What has been done?
- What has to be done?

Planning:
- What needs to be done to achieve the goals?
- Have you confirmed that everyone knows what is going on?
- Have you taken into account contingencies?
- Have you viewed the venue?
- Have you prepared your Presentation Pack?
- Have you arranged the materials?

Execution:
- Guide the audience
- Give the delivery
- Direct the feedback
- Ensure the follow up work is understood

Review or monitor:
- Interpret response
- Alter delivery
- Ensure follow up work is carried out
- Find out how the training has helped 3-6 months on

Some additional tips for presentations or seminars
The objective is what you must achieve. It is not how long you talk but the fact that you achieve what you set out to achieve.

During my political days I had a very good friend who thought going into Europe was the worst thing that could happen to the U.K. At a conference, someone put in a speaker slip for him to speak in favour of a 'United Europe'. Instead of my friend declining and saying there had been a mistake he ventured up to the platform in front of everyone and stood and started to speak...Chairman, Ladies and Gentlemen, I would like to speak on everything that is good about a United States of Europe... his voice trailed off and he remained standing behind the podium. Our initial thoughts were that he has experienced stage fright and forgotten his words but he remained quite still, just looking at the audience. Murmuring in the audience started and after about 30 seconds people started to laugh. He finished his silence with 'thank you Chairman, Ladies and Gentlemen' and went and sat down to raptures of applause. He achieved sending his message without saying a word! How is that for effective communication?

Finally, remember the recency effect. Summarise your key points at the end and have clear closing lines as it is those closing lines which the audience will remember for longer than any other piece of your presentation. Make sure each word counts.

SECTION 3
Success Techniques

CHAPTER 13

The Magic Factor

The state of the mind

A *positive attitude*

There is much written about PMA – Positive Mental Attitude, and so I would recommend you look up excellent authors and read up on the subject. This next section, however, is designed to give you a taster and communicate how important a positive mental attitude is when you are trying to achieve the Advanced Power State and yet constantly surrounded by negativity.

Negativity breeds negativity. Negativity destroys and yet as humans, we tend more and more to become negative within ourselves. Can you take on the challenge to counter negativity when you see it, whether it is your immediate friends, work colleagues, television or anywhere else? Can you turn negativity into positivity? Negativity drains our energy. Beat back negativity and convert the negativity into positivity.

By being positive you will continue to be enthusiastic long after others have faded. You will maintain your energy, and your health will be stronger. Remember enthusiasm is one of the key elements of the success equation discussed in Chapter 1.

Problems will cease to exist or be greatly reduced and will not weigh down your mind. So how do we start being positive?

Firstly, as with the V.A.P.E.R, Vision, Analysis, Planning, Execution and Review, you will find that we need to define our purpose, our goal, and our vision. So before we do that, I would like you to carry out the following exercises:

Get yourself a piece of paper, and on a fresh sheet write down the following:

What you think your ideal life would be like? What would you be doing? Where would you like to be?

If you just won £10 million in the lottery, what would you do with it? What would you stop doing?

If you were told by the doctor you had just two years to live and you received a huge cash sum, what would you do?

Write down the ten most wanted things you want to:

- Do
- Buy

What do you want people to remember you for? If, after you were dead, someone was asked about you, what would you want them to say?

This may be a strange way to start to think positively but it begins to give you some positive direction.

Decide now to cast out negativity from your life.

Write it down on your list of goals.

From the time I ran my own company, I tried, within the company, to take out 'office politics' and change negativity to positivity. Many times, things went wrong. We always had things to put right but instead of everyone thinking of them as problems I wanted them to think more positively. I wanted them to see problems as something they could solve, a puzzle, an opportunity to show their ability to overcome issues that exist. I therefore forbade anyone from saying the word 'problem'! It started as a joke but even the laughter changed the concept of a negative problem by reframing the issue to a possibility to improve and do something special and an opportunity for them to show everyone their skills.

Whilst I did not achieve a full ban on the word, people tried and eventually, in most cases, succeeded in reframing a problem to be a positive challenge, something they could work on and achieve.

We started saying 'We don't have problems, just challenges and opportunities' and then all laughed together.

If I come to you and say I have a problem, you may subconsciously say, 'Well up yours Mate, I have loads of problems.' Hopefully it is only a subconscious thought. I am sure you would not do it in the conscious mind and would never say it out loud, however, you cannot help your subconscious mind relating it to your problems. Remember: negativity breeds further negativity and it affects your whole body, your health and your life blood.

With a positive mental attitude you have the ability to achieve anything you want. However, it is not enough to say it. You must believe it and have this firmly in your mindset.

The first place to start is the use of your language. Try to banish negative words and create positive rather than negative images.

Take an example:

Visualise the next two sentences. What do you see in your mind's eye?

'Don't leave the room in a mess'.

Now,

'Leave the room in a mess'.

From the words, the meaning of one statement is exactly the opposite of the other but from the visual angle, they create the same overall image. The subconscious mind will keep the bad image and when it brings it to the conscious mind it will add the 'don't' part, as long as it remembers the trigger to do that.

So how about rephrasing it to:

'Leave your room tidy'.

Do you now visualize a room that is tidy and in your subconscious mind, have you set yourself a positive target or reinforcement?

Say 'Don't think of a snake'.

Naughty, naughty! How many of you have thought of a snake? The visual image is the idea; the concept is what we remember.

When the body comes into contact with negativity, whether it is written, spoken or just body language, the chemicals in the body react a certain way, using neuropeptides, and these change how you feel. The more negativity there is, the more your body loses its energy and vitality, and the more you are likely to become sick.

One of the ways I combat negativity is by looking for it. It becomes a game, 'oh there is some more, I'll avoid that too!'

Get a newspaper or watch the news. I suggest that the majority of those stories are negative and are there to invoke some emotion and it will usually be fear! It is called entertainment. However, you need to identify these things and frame them in a more positive world.

A quote from the West End musical 'Time – The Musical' is relevant here. 'Remember: the one thing you have full control over is your thinking' and so you do.

There is a concept here that many have difficulty in accepting, and in my numerous discussions with people, to this day they find it difficult to accept. A thought in your head is real whether it is actually exists or is imaginary. It is the conscious mind that tags the image, the thought, with the additional information saying 'remember that this thought is imaginary'. If, when the image is seen, that tag does not get stored, then the brain will accept the image as real, in not only the subconscious mind but also the conscious mind. The key is that whether it is real or not, the body will react to it in the same way. If you watch a scary film your heart will jump and your body will go into stress at the scary bits. Is that not what happens in real life? The hormones will be excreted automatically. They are there to help you deal with the situation and the mind will prepare you to be ready to flee or fight.

I once saw a seminar where one of the presenters asked a random person from the audience (and I verified later that they were random), to say a quick positive sentence over and over again whilst holding their arm out at shoulder height to the side. They did this and whilst they were doing it, the man asked them to hold the arm in place whilst he tried to push it down to his side. It was very hard to do! He then asked the person to say a negative reinforcing set of words over and over again and did the same thing. It was very easy with the negative reinforcement. Out of interest, I tried the same thing and it worked, which helped prove to me the point of how important positivity is in our lives.

How people react

In an earlier chapter we were talking about how we want people react to us. When we are negative, people react badly. They:

* Often look away
* Avoid eye contact
* In fact, avoid any contact at all

If you are positive then people will come and want to talk to you. At the bar, scowl and see how many people pass the time of day with conversation. Now go to the bar with a beaming smile; I bet someone will talk to you! (Is this where I put in the disclaimer that if in a bar, you have to drink responsibly?)

People will talk to, want to be around and be in contact with those who think positively because it comes out in the body language and all interaction.

Make yourself positive

How else then can you make yourself more positive? We have already looked at clear objectives as vision keeps you focussed. We have also agreed to avoid people who are negative as energy is easily sapped from enthusiastic individuals. If you cannot avoid the negative people, then understand their negative energy and counter it in your mind. Do not let them pass on their negative energy to you and make sure you get sufficient breaks with positive people, otherwise eventually you will succumb without realizing it.

Another way is to increase your self-discipline further. Stick to your guns and don't let others cause you to deviate from your path. Listen to your heart and your subconscious. Let them be the judge.

Give yourself strong reinforcement. Say over and over, 'I can do that'. Banish the words 'can't', 'won't', 'shan't' and 'don't' from your dictionary. Insert instead, 'of course', 'when', 'I can do it', 'yes' etc.

Take time before doing something to imagine you having done it and the success it brings. See it in your mind!

Read a book called *How to Stop Worrying and Start Living* by

Dale Carnegie as worrying is negative and 90% of worries are imaginary. Remember, even if they are imaginary, they drain your life force. Either way, 90% of things you worry about will never happen and the rest will almost always be less serious than you imagine them to be.

In addition, never ever worry about something that has happened or been done, or will happen if you can do nothing about it. It is a complete waste of your time, energy and life force.

Take a list of items you are worried about and write them down. Write down how you expect the situation to work out. Update the outcomes and compare your expectations some time later perhaps a day, week or month. Prove the 90% rule.

Intuition

Many people talk about the 'sixth sense'. I believe intuition is linked in with the subconscious and can easily be defined as a 'sixth sense'. Certainly it is a tool which if worked with and trained, can achieve immense results.

Intuition is hard to describe but to me it is the inner voice, it is the feeling you have. Some would call it your 'gut feeling'.

How is this feeling arrived at?

It is not anything you can touch, taste, smell, see, and hear. That is why it can be defined as the 'sixth sense'. You just know it to be right. It is a force, an inner force inside and outside of us.

Your intuition works by the use of the subconscious directing the conscious mind. The subconscious manipulates data at millions of executions per second. This direction, along with the sensory inputs, now add together using your Personal Knowledge Base to give you that intuition.

I have noticed that the intuition gets stronger with a deeper Personal Knowledge Base. This continues in my studies to be a very important factor in achieving success.

How many times have you said 'I thought that would happen'? Many, I feel sure. Perhaps, because you have seen it happen before or something similar, or something that is not similar, that your brain guides you to that conclusion even though it quite often seems unexplainable.

Either way, it is that Personal Knowledge Base of information which once again is shown to be important.

Intuition uses the subconscious mind and we have said it uses the sensory inputs as well. It is not hard to realize that it therefore uses the whole body to create this sensory 'net'. This leads us on to more questions for discussion, which are 'What is the mind?', 'Where do the mind and body split?' and 'Are they split at all?' These are interesting questions which many scientists are currently in debate over.

So how do we improve intuition? Many of the items covered in this book will help. However, I have found it helps to observe and think more laterally about things. It is about understanding possibilities and probabilities, something we will cover more of in a later chapter, about risk.

So here are a couple of fun things to do for lateral thinking. Try to get a book to assist in lateral thinking, if nothing else, they are often fun.

Answer me this:

Jim and Elizabeth had dinner together for the first time in 8 months although they have been happily married for 2 years; explain?

Two orange juices, two lemonades, a bottle of Beck's, a Grolsch and a packet of crisps cost me £20.70. I have the exact money in a £20 note and two coins; one of the coins is not a 50p piece. What are the two coins?

See if you can get the answers?

So to help improve intuition you have to look at the following:

- Be strong in mind and body
- Be healthy in mind and body
- Eat the right foods, tone the body and mind
- Be relaxed and positive minded about surroundings to let the ideas flow
- Work laterally and open the mind to possibilities and probabilities
- Use imagination
- Have a good Personal Knowledge Base
- Use the subconscious and enhance its abilities

Learn to listen and trust your inner voice.

Imagination

Imagination is very much linked into intuition. At Disney World in Florida I came across their Kingdom of Imagination at the EPCOT centre. I found it a fascinating and thought-provoking place. It was a place where I could go on my own and just think about things. I could explore my own imagination.

Children at school are constantly criticised when daydreaming but it is this use of the imagination we need to encourage, admittedly perhaps not in the middle of a maths lesson, but then again, why not?

> *I ended up being really good at maths, getting a grade A at O-level and moving on to engineering, however, all I can remember of our maths lessons was John Moss's holiday slides. That was certainly using imagination because to this day, I remain good at maths.*

I found that often I was not able to create, even with a blank sheet of paper in front of me. In the end, I found some Mind Mapping software which allowed me to write in the middle what I wanted to create and then the brain did the rest. I went from being unimaginative to very imaginative in less than 3 years.

Using imagination is thinking 'beyond the box'. At work they will pay you more for ideas that are new, are innovative, and that work.

Life Force

Over the years I have come to believe that each of us has an internal force. It is built up of natural substances and involves nature. Sometimes this life force is full of energy and sometimes it is not. Sometimes I have felt powerful, strong and enthusiastic and ready to take on the world, and sometimes I have felt weak and unable to perform at my best. It is likely that much of this is to do with the chemicals inside us and yet I believe there is more to it than that.

There are rational reasons for what makes the wind blow, for things to grow. However, this nature may well be the life force. The Greeks and Egyptians used to worship all sorts of Gods, the sun, the sea, the wind etc. Perhaps these are the items that make the life force. In my observation, the mental faculty is linked completely with the body, and with nature.

It is accepted in the UK that the majority of people will feel stronger and happier in the spring and summer than in the winter. There are more deaths recorded in the winter when it is colder and darker. Perhaps the life force I see is just nature or is it our soul? What is our soul? Is it our mind?

I am not going to discuss God and religion in this book as this is a personal and private thing. However, ask yourself the question, why is the wind blowing? How did we come to live? What started it all off? Why do the trees blossom? etc. You cannot answer these questions. No one can.
But faith can be applied in everything you do. Faith means believing even when you do not have the evidence to prove it.

I believe, and there is evidence to support, that there is a life force, something more than we know, and I believe it is linked with the mind. Why can people do amazing things when life is threatening their loved ones? This is because they call on a life force, perhaps something they call God.

This life force or maybe God goes under many names but there is definitely something out there.

Mother Nature, the subconscious, God; I am not sure!

Some people even say the mind is our whole body and the brain just the central processing unit. All I can say is there is something out there which I cannot explain. Scientists try and often believe they can explain but to me it still exists and it is this life force that can give you the energy and enthusiasm to go on and achieve great things.

If there is a force and you can call on this force to help, it would be very powerful even if it is imaginary. If it helps you to focus the mind and body to achieve then you should use it and call on it to help. How many times have you wanted that extra bit of strength to go on or that extra energy to see it through? Has it been granted?

Why not try it yourself. You will be amazed at its power.

It was quite funny because *Star Wars* used the words 'feel the force Luke'. Well maybe they were on to something. If you call on that force, and give yourself firm reassuring verbalisation then you WILL achieve your goals. If nothing else this focusses you and your inner energy. Remember that the last UK census has 'Jedi', put down by thousands, as a religion!

Not accepting the status quo

Change is vital in life, indeed it is what I call a constant. Change is happening all of the time and you can either get on board or get off. If you get off, you get left behind, however, there is another possibility here. Instead of just saying 'get on board' you can lead the change and the best way is to constantly challenge the status quo. Constantly review: What is happening? How? Where? Why things are being done? And constantly look for better ways of achieving things.

The status quo is old. The status quo is gone. Look for the next change, the next thing that will improve your ability to achieve.

Huge self-confidence and assertion

Self-confidence is a major factor in your relationships with others and indeed perception. It is vital to build your self-confidence by building up that knowledge and experience and by believing that you can do it.

> *Someone once said to me 'If another human being can do something then I can, if I learn the same as they have and I practise like they do'.*

It is true you can do anything you want to if you prepare, so long as you do not have some kind of condition that prevents you.

I always get stopped in shops and asked questions, just things such as 'What time do you close?' or 'Where is the so-and-so?' The reason is: I have an air of self-confidence. I normally look the part and my body language emanates an air of being in charge.

That self-confidence comes from experience, from running a shop, from preparing what I do. We all start off the same but it is the ones that firstly show confidence and secondly are confident that will do well.

Many people have fallen because they are unsure.

> *I once went for a major job and the interviewer said to me 'Are you sure you can do the job?' and without thinking I said 'I know I can do the job, it's whether I want to that is the question'.*

> *When I left the interview I could not believe I had said it! But I did because I was confident it was true. I got the job!*

Attention to detail

More and more, I find that people are looking for an easy life and they do so at the expense of shoddy work. Yes, everyone is under pressure but attention to detail is vital to survive. It is almost always the case that the devil is in the detail, and my approach of 'questioning to the void' has always been a major part of ensuring I get to the detail.

When doing work, attention to detail, and preparation, are key drivers to achieving success. It also helps people trust you and what you do.

It is only by trusting and being trusted that you will you get on.

Credibility

Credibility is another key factor in achieving the Advanced Power State. You need to be credible and some of the ways of achieving that are:

- Being confident
- Having a good track record
- Having a good reputation
- Demonstrating the ability at whatever you are doing
- Having the knowledge and experience required
- Having the personality that drives the success
- Being good with communications
- Excelling in the techniques of the Advanced Power State

Ownership & responsibility

If you want to succeed, if you want to be better than the next person, you need to step forward and take ownership and responsibility for what you are doing and for any teams you are leading. You may get it wrong, but it still shows strength of character to accept praise humbly and to accept criticism gracefully. Ultimately it is only by taking ownership that you project yourself forward, that you start to stand out as the high flyer you are to become.

Continuous improvement

This is an old phrase now but for me, still as important as the day it was first used. As a person, if you do not continue to learn, continue to improve yourself and your mind, you will slip back and other people will take your place.

> *When I left school I did not go to university immediately, I went out to work and became a store manager with a UK national chain of stores, and then a high-flyer in the head office of a retail company. We implemented systems all over the country and then I came to the realization that I wanted to know more, to be more. I went back to university and realized that I had lost the ability to study. It took a complete term to bring myself back in line and I vowed there and then that each year I would set myself a learning task and achieve it, and to this day I have and continue to do so.*

Systematic thinking

Orderly and structured thinking are more likely to bring you success than disorderly thinking. Now some may say that with art, it should not be structured and on that I will not comment. I can say, from my experience, that systematic thinking at work will make you incredibly powerful, and if you can achieve that then you will have taken an important step to the Advanced Power State.

Once you have achieved good solid systematic thinking why not try systemic thinking, which will take you a step even higher.

If you want to know about these ways of thinking there are many texts written about this.

Bounce back from lessons learned and bad experiences

One of the bigger things that successful people will tell you is that you will make mistakes, that we all make mistakes and to be successful you must learn from them and bounce back.

Take positive elements from the worst situations and vow never to fall into the same trap again. Learn from those bad experiences and ensure that next time they become good experiences.

Anticipate

In a later chapter we will look at risk, and perhaps anticipation is partially linked. It is important to play through scenarios in your head to anticipate the effect, or likely, possible effects of the actions that you or others are embarking on.

The more you carry out the 'What if?' questioning, the more you will automatically anticipate things and the more you get to know people and their world view, the more you will anticipate their actions. Also, the more knowledge and experience you have, the more you will anticipate what could possibly happen.

Learn to anticipate by thinking more laterally and carrying out all of the suggested learning points from this book.

The subconscious mind

We have touched on the subconscious mind many times so far in this book and I would like to explain its significance here.

So firstly answer the question: what does a cat like to do? Play, is of course the answer! So what does the subconscious mind like to do? Think! In fact it is the only thing it does, and it is what it was created for. That is what it does 24 hours a day, whether you like it or not.

Hang on then! 24 hours a day. Whilst we are only awake with the conscious brain for somewhere between 16 and 18 hours, the subconscious works 24 hours a day and that is a full 25% more time than the conscious mind can work.

So that means that if you can train the subconscious to work with you, then you can be a minimum of 25% more effective and given that we do not use the conscious or the subconscious mind very well, then it could be a vast improvement in processessing capability.

It does not stop there, though. The subconscious is infinitely more powerful than the conscious brain. It is really a natural force to be reckoned with. How many things can you think about at any one time?

Most people would say only one and they probably can – in the conscious mind. However, with training you can increase the conscious mind to a maximum of about eight according to studies done in the USA.

The subconscious can think of thousands of strands putting them altogether and improving intuition and lateral thinking all of the time at work, rest and play.

Training the subconscious to work with you is a very effective way of heading towards the Advanced Power State. Remember it is working anyway and the key is to get it to work with you to achieve your objectives.

People will tell you it makes them tired if they try to learn just before going to bed. That is simply not true. All you are doing is focussing on something you want to think about rather than something you initially do not. The only time it will make you tired is if you are going to bed worrying about something.

So to get the most out of your conscious and subconscious mind you need to:

- Have good light
- Have a low sugar diet
- Eat balanced meals
- Be well hydrated
- Have low stress levels

You need to concentrate the conscious mind onto a single subject, continually coming back to that subject. Put the topic onto your office wall or somewhere where you spend a considerable amount of time. The subconscious mind also works better in a relaxed state. It may be worth you having a warm bath or meditating, whatever it is that relaxes you – then you can put the positive thoughts into your conscious mind knowing that your subconscious is likely to be more receptive to taking these on board and increasing the allocated brain power to solving the challenges.

If you do not choose to work your subconscious for your benefit then it will work anyway and it just might work on things that are little or no interest to you. The choice, of course, is entirely up to you.

So tune the subconscious mind by relaxing and then using all of your sensory inputs, including the conscious mind, to focus the subconscious on what you need it to think about and contemplate that this might be the life force, this might be the 'sixth sense'.

Remember though that if your body is unwell, or you do not have well-balanced chemical reactions within your body and brain, your subconscious will not run at optimum capacity. It is up to you to resolve this and to get it to work towards your goals.

Have you ever awoken in the morning after going to bed with a major decision hanging over you and thought 'That's it. That is the answer'. I have many times. That is the subconscious processing through the night.

Dreaming again is another way of using the subconscious, perhaps even with the conscious mind. This can be random or can be focussed to work to help solve the challenges we are meeting rather than random thought processes.

Just remember that your subconscious is always helping you achieve your conscious demands. If you think negatively, the life force around you will help you to achieve your negative goals.

If you think and continue to talk positively, if you have a positive mindset you will convince the subconscious to help you achieve your positive goals.

See things from different points of view

Everyone has their own point of view. This view is created out of the Personal Knowledge Base and the experiences they have gained through their lives. It is important for you to always put yourself into their shoes and remove yourself from your shoes.

This sometimes means doing some research into the person whose point of view you want to know about. It is perhaps worth getting to know them better, what have they done in the past and where have they lived. All of this will improve your ability to see it from their point of view. Obviously you can never actually see their point of view but so many things depend upon you understanding that there is a different opinion and trying to understand it that it is worth the work.

Focus

Direction is a part of the success equation at the beginning of this book. The ability to focus really is allied to this. Once you have the direction, you must be focussed, you must decide to make the sacrifices you need to achieve your goal and to pay the price for that success. An Olympic athlete trains for 4 years and often many more to win an Olympic games. They give up an incredible amount of their life, sometimes training almost all of their waking life and eating exactly what they need to succeed. Focus on your objectives, on the end game and it will help you to achieve that higher level of success.

Giving that added value

I have heard for many years the phrase of giving 'added value', and it is only since running my own company that I really came to understand it. Where do you 'add value'? To what you are doing, to your boss or to your family? If you 'add value', great. Write it down and now write down where you add significant value. It is about doing that extra bit. It is about achieving more than you or anyone expects and it is extremely important in life.

I visited San Francisco a number of years ago and wanted to send a few postcards. I went to buy some stamps and the cashier duly gave me the stamps. As I was turning to leave he said 'I'll tell you what. Let me give you some of these airmail stickers. Oh and would you like a bag to keep those out of the rain?'

I left and felt pleased. When I tried to analyse why, I realised that they had given me 'added value' in a way that made me feel I got something extra. In my analysis they probably were supposed to give the airmail stickers and a little bag too!

I still felt good.

You need to do that little bit more than everyone else, or a lot more.

Be a doer

Actions speak louder than words. I have and continue to hear people saying that they are going to do this, that etc. What I really want to hear is 'I have done this' and 'have done that'. Doers achieve, talkers rarely do!

Success can only be achieved by doing. To talk is fine but to do is success. So keep things positively moving forward and cut out the meetings and the talk.

Be a farmer

No, I do not mean success will come if you go and attend to cows and sheep but I do mean that you reap what you sow! This clearly means that if you put down good seed and look after the seed you will grow a superb crop. If, on the other hand, you put down cheap seed and do not nurture it, you will harvest a poor crop.

Now I learned this saying when I was at school and to me it means 'do things without the thought of reward and reward will happen anyway'. For me it is also described by another saying:

'What you put into life you get out' – a motto I have lived with all of my life.

Work hard and you will achieve more than if you are lazy. The harder you work the more successful you will become.

Discipline

Discipline is critical. Doing something because it is the right thing to do, even if it is difficult or may be unpleasant, is important. Your own self-discipline is also important, going against something that draws you to pleasure because you know it is the right thing to do.

Discipline for you is important!

CHAPTER 14

The Growing Machine

I ran a company for a number of years and in doing so learnt to appreciate that there are many different aspects to running one:

- Sales
- Marketing
- Finances
- Research and development

Looking at an individual, the same could be said. We don't really work for anyone else other than ourselves. I have to sell myself and market myself to get the best jobs and opportunities. I have a budget at home and I have to live within that budget. I carry out learning all of the time, setting myself targets each year, and I work. In fact, almost every aspect of a company can be compared with an individual and so keeping that individual, keeping me, in the best condition is the best way to achieve success.

Most people, including me, know what we should do and yet we don't do it. Either way this is a reminder as to how to get the most from your body, from your own company.

If you owned a factory or a company and it is taken 'off line', shut down, what can you make or do? Nothing and the same applies to your body. If you are sick, you can provide nothing and whilst there is insurance and safety-nets, essentially your company (you), will have nothing to deliver. If it stays like that for long enough it will be very hard to bring it back up to its optimum operating level. Your body and thus your health are vital to success.

Happy or healthy in body and mind

To be healthy in body and mind means doing exercise, anything from walking to more aerobic exercise. The best bet being to do some of each. To keep the body fit, it is said that you should work out for longer than 20-30 minutes at least 3 times a week. I recommend longer than that. We should be looking at 40 minutes at between 60-80% of your personal maximum heart rate. Something a gym can advise you on.

A healthy body will help deal with the stressors mentioned earlier. It is recognized that stress relief comes from:

- Good nutrition
- The required amount of sleep (which varies from person to person)
- A fair-paced work level
- Regular exercise and general fitness

The mind also needs looking after. It is important to take opportunities to relax the mind and the body. There are things such as yoga, but just plain and simple meditation will also act as a good exercise for building the mind and the body.

Eat the right foods. Well I do not do very well here and I am sure many of you are the same but it will help your health if you eat healthily.

Rest and relaxation themselves prove absolutely vital. A holiday is a must, and this may not be a holiday away with the family it may be a private holiday on your own, away from it all!

A few years back when I was the managing director of a business, I had been working very hard doing all sorts of hours around the clock to keep things moving on. I also was trying to keep a social life.

After splitting with a girlfriend, I decided to take a holiday. I had not had one in two years so on 28th December I gave my credit card to Thomas Cook and asked them to take me to the sun for the first week in January; they took me to Israel.

There are many stories I could tell you about it but suffice it to say I was tired and exhausted.

It took 4 days for me to recover and relax and it then was almost time to return.

I came back refreshed and ready to take on the challenges that lay ahead. I was fully charged with lots of ideas and I had taken a step back and shown my employees that they too could work on their own.

Health is about eating right and it is recommended as part of the balanced diet that we eat five portions of fruit and vegetables per person each day. Additionally, we should keep our level of meat to 2 or 3 times a week and we should have more fish in our diet.

We should drink, approximately, 8 average glasses of water a day and more in the summer. We should keep avoid caffeine which takes water out of the body. We should also limit our alcohol.

We should eat a hearty breakfast and lunch with a lighter snack at dinner time.

Your body is continually undergoing change from the moment you are conceived until the moment that you die. When you are growing up, your body goes through many different cycles. In addition we do different activities. When I was at school we were very active from the exercise point of view, not just in the playground but also in the PE lessons and extracurricular activities. When you leave school, college or university, your exercise will often slow down. At the same time through the ages of about 21 to 23 your body stops growing and the body just replaces and repairs itself. When these things happen your metabolic rate changes accordingly. At these times you need less food, calories, to maintain the body and this is at the same time your exercise level has dropped and so you need less food to cover the usage from the exercise.

This leads to an imbalance between the calories you eat and the calories used by the body, which eventually ends up with the excess calories stored as fat, and we put on weight.

If you forget this fact then you will become more and more fat, and thus want to do less, and therefore use less energy and get more and more fat... it becomes a vicious circle. The secret is to have sufficient exercise and eat a balanced diet. Easier said than done, I will admit, but if you are committed to a healthy body then you need to work at it.

The less you follow this advice the more the ability to do things and the motivation to do them decays.

Remember the mind and body are linked and external factors affect both. If the sun shines we feel better and if we feed the body with the correct balance of nutrients we will feel more energetic.

Remember as well that it is better to eat additional complex carbohydrates, such as wholewheat pasta than sugar. Simple carbohydrates such as sugar enter the blood stream very quickly and cause insulin to be released. The speed of the sugar inwards causes the insulin to be released in a higher quantity than required and thus balance goes out and between 30 and 60 minutes after having the sugar you feel low and your energy is reduced.

There are many books on diet and eating correctly to enable you to go out and research this further.

Exercise gives you life

Exercise is recognised as being essential to keep the body in good form. It can relieve stress and it ensures a better blood flow, leading to more oxygen to the brain and muscles. Bear in mind that this oxygen is life to the brain and starving it of oxygen will not help it to perform better.

The body is a complex machine but it is recognised that (with the exception of a very few, on medical grounds), aerobic exercise is a must, giving an all-round better feeling and stronger body and mind if carried out regularly.

Don't overdo it though. Start with a little bit and build up the work every few days. If you are doing something everyday ensure that you have at least 2 in 7 days for your body to repair itself.

Regular aerobic exercise will give you more energy and enthusiasm – something that is in the success equation. A stronger body will protect you better from illnesses and speed recovery if you are taken ill, and a stronger mind gives you greater capacity to perform.

Go and join a gym today or read up on exercise, what you can do and how it can help you and if necessary just start with simple exercise like walking.

Build on your energy

We know that health is important and we know that you are what you eat. There are many things that it would be better to steer clear of, but my view has often been that most things, in moderation, give you the balance you need. There are some items, however, in our everyday diet that many nutritional experts claim are poisons. These are known as the five white poisons and since I found out about them I have tried to reduce my intake of them:

- Sugar
- Salt
- Flour
- Milk
- White rice

Look at how many foods contain these substances! Try to reduce the amount of each you have. It is not easy.

Muscle

Our bodies are made up of many elements: skin; blood, water, organs, muscle and bones being the six major elements. I want to take muscle and look at it further.

Muscle is the means by which you move your bones and by which those bones are held in place. Without muscles you would be just a pile of bones, and other elements would be unable to move. So how do we build muscles?

Muscles are built by using them. The more you use them the more they grow. It is recommended that to build muscle you work the muscle up to just beyond your comfortable level. This is called 'overload'! If you do this then next time you come to use those muscles they will be able to achieve a little bit more. If you continue to do this, the muscles will continue to grow. Not too much overload or you will injure yourself. You want to go just beyond what is comfortable. If on the other hand you do not use muscles for between 48 and 72 hours, then they start to go into regression and disintegrate. It is therefore important that you use your muscles at least three times a week and carry out exercise, be that running walking, aerobic classes, swimming. Whatever it is, if you fail to get sufficient exercise during the day in whatever you are doing for work or education, then it needs to be supplemented.

This principle of working the organs works for the brain too. The more you use it, the more it grows and the more you can use it. The less you use it, the more it will close down and be less effective. The Advanced Power State needs you to use it and continue to use it to its maximum capability.

Acute senses

Keep those senses toned up. Make sure you are not looking at the world go by, but make sure you see and feel and understand the world as it goes by. Take breaks from your work, some people call these 'brain breaks'. This will help you keep the body working at maximum capacity and you will be able do more and achieve more.

> *My brother went on a cruise a few years ago around the Caribbean. He hired a satellite telephone!*

Modern communications make this so much easier with Blackberries and texting devices, but make sure you get sufficient breaks. Your body needs it.

> *I picked up a card a few weeks ago and on it was written 'Everyday is a place I have never been before'.*

Stress and illness

We have already looked at the subject of negativity and that negative thinking brings the body down and sucks the life force from the body. Stress does the same. They both make us feel at dis-ease. This not at ease is where I believe the word disease came from. So how do we make the body work better and be more effective?

I would firstly like to briefly go over the causes of stress. Whilst banishing negativity is important, controlling stress is as important.

There are seven well known stressors. They are:

- Culture
- Demands
- Control
- Support
- Relationships
- Role
- Change

Culture
It has to be said that different people belong in different cultures and it is important that you feel at ease with the culture you are working in. Do you prefer the outside with casual work patterns, or do you prefer everything detailed and planned to the point where you can only take tea breaks at specific times? If there is a mismatch in culture it will constantly raise your stress level.

Demands
If the demands on you are unreasonable for you, or for your ability to achieve them, then that will put additional stress on you. Different people have different levels of demand that they can cope with before they begin to feel stressed, and it is not just about work. Stress comes from all walks of life and it is the accumulation of all of those demands that can lead to stress.

Control

Control is an important factor in life. It is recognized that for most people the more control they have over their lives and what they do, the less stress they will find themselves in. This control applies to security, money, work and in fact any element of life. Your level of stress relates to how much you feel in control.

Support

Support is another stressor. If you are heavily supported then you will be less stressed. Whether that support is at home, at work, or in any part of your life, the more support you have the less stressed you will be.

Relationships

Relationships, for me, also tie into belonging. If there is friction or anger within any of your relationships then there will be additional stress. If you are being harassed, bullied or picked on, then the level of stress will increase.

Role

The role you play at work or at leisure time is an important factor in stress. In the main, it is not about what your role is, but about understanding what is expected of you. It is about the level of boredom in your role, how repetitive your role is, and whether you are happy with that role. Any of these can cause additional stress.

Change

Finally, one of the big stressors and something you really need to change from within is change itself. Change leads to stress in many situations. Now often this stress comes from the unknown and the more you know about the change, the less the stress.

However, I would suggest that change leads to worry and worry can be a huge contributor to stress. Get over worry, embrace the unknown, as it is out of the unknown that true success can be shaped.

To me, pressure is good. Having deadlines for things to achieve, targets to get, is important. However, pressure becomes stress at the point you can no longer handle all of the pressure. Like life, it is a balance. If you have clear markers or behavioural patterns which allow you to understand how much pressure you can take then that is fine, but even with all of those in place, for goodness' sake – take a holiday!

If you can understand stress, then you stand a good chance at optimizing pressure and keeping stress out. So look at the stressors above and see how they relate to your work and leisure environments.

Budgeting time and money

There are two precious resources I will touch on next: money and time. To some extent they are interchangeable. You trade your time for money, which we call work. The higher your value to an organisation, the higher the amount of money you will earn. It is therefore important to consider time availability and thus ensure that priorities are given to the things that will lead you towards your goals and not just wasted on anything. Discipline has a part to play here. A disciplined person will not waste time and will use every available minute. Learn to use your time wisely.

If you look at the day, it usually is something like this:

- We work for 8 hours
- We sleep for 8 hours

It is the other 8 hours that makes the difference. If you can use that additional 8 hours as well as the 8 hours at work more effectively than the next person then you will be a further step to being more successful.

We have already covered a number of ways of doing this:

- Reading faster
- Remembering better
- Being focussed on goals
- Using your subconscious mind

There are other obvious ways; by using true time management principles, planning your time, monitoring your wastage and realising that when someone uses your time and it is not to your objective, then they are taking time away from the things you need to do or from your time with your family.

Where money is concerned, it is also a key resource. Like any good company, you have your accounts. Understand your income and outgoings and put something aside for your insurance and for your research and development, that is your training and education.

Even if it is a small amount to start with, save a little a week and as you become more successful, you will be able to increase the amount saved. How much you think you should save is up to you. I would suggest 5 to 10% of your income.

Spend your money on things that are in line with your objectives and again define your priorities. Remember to have fun as well!

Having a little bit of money saved reduces your stress and worry in case something happens and you cannot earn for a while!

CHAPTER 15

Risk

My definition of risk is:

'Risk is an uncertain event which, should it occur, will have an effect on the achievement of objectives.'

Risk management is allied to change and change is constant in life; change is all around us. Risk is about seeing what impact the change is going to have and assessing the size of that impact and the possibility that the impact will happen. It is linked in with anticipating what is going on.

These are fancy words and many may ask why you would put this in a book about success. The answer is that the ability to assess risk, and to either embrace the change or mitigate the negative effects, is critical in achieving the Advanced Power State.

For many people risk management will conjure up all sorts of processes. Some may even consider it as just a big paper exercise but risk, to me, is about constantly, and eventually automatically, considering what is going to happen.

At work I once wrote on the whiteboard:

'We need to know what is going to happen before it happens'.

Many of those present said it was impossible, but really that is what risk is about. If you know what is going to happen before the person next to you, then you stand a better chance of being able to gain from it, whether that is taking advantage of an opportunity or mitigating something harmful.

So learn to follow the simple risk process, on paper if you wish or in your mind.

- Identify the risk(s)
- Document them if you wish
- Validate them
- Assess and evaluate them
- Think and execute ways of dealing with each risk
- Continue to monitor the situation

The idea is not to make this a long process but to take the example of someone crossing the road:

Identify the risks: a vehicle may come and hit you or you may slip if the road is slippery. Those two are the first that come to mind.

Validate them: the likelihood of a car hitting you is high on roads and so the risk is very valid and perhaps if it has not been raining it is unlikely that you will slip, but it is still a risk.

Assess and evaluate: what type of road is it? How fast is the road? Is it a busy road? What time of day is it? Can you hear any vehicles? (which does not stop a bicycle or an electric car being there!) These criteria can help you assess the likelihood that a vehicle might hit you and the impact of being hit.

Firstly a through road would make it very busy and increase the likelihood of a car hitting you. A faster road would again increase the likelihood but certainly increase the impact enormously.

Think and execute a way of dealing with the risk: you might not cross the road, if it is too busy. You might look for nearby traffic lights or an underpass.

Finally, you should monitor the situation. If it is busy at a particular time of day then perhaps later would be better for crossing safely.

So risk is more than just health and safety. It is about seeing an opportunity and grasping it. An easy example would be shares. If you believed that a particular industry is going to do well then you may risk your money looking for a greater return. That return would be the increase in price and the return when you sold them, along with the likelihood that the shares will go up!

People think too much that risk is just the negative side. Without risk there is no reward.

So how do you get better at risk? Well again Knowledge and Experience have a major part to play. The more knowledge and experience you have the more likely you are to have come across a similar situation and be able to understand the possible impacts and then assess the likelihood. This leads on to the fact that lateral thinking helps. If you saw someone having trouble swimming in a calm swimming pool, then seeing someone go swimming in the sea with big waves would let you understand that the risk is here as well.

Knowledge and experience are the two major factors in understanding risk.
Applying that knowledge and experience to understand risk are as important, as most people rarely think about risk, and they miss what could happen, and they miss great opportunities.

It is important to analyse the probability and impact. Initially, if risk is relatively new to you it will probably be done on paper. However, eventually, like anything, if you train your brain to do it and practise enough, then it becomes automatic and your mind follows through the steps of risk without even being aware of it.

Some of the ways I calculate risk are:

- Having a regular checklist of past risks
- Having categories to look at
- Talking to experts
- Brainstorming
- Using analogous comparisons
- Looking at areas of vulnerability

There are others but even starting out with these seven areas will help you to frame risk correctly.

So to determine the level of risk I assign a number between 1 and 5. For 1, a low risk and 5, a high risk. I then do the same to impact and assign 1 for a low impact and 5 for a high impact.

When you multiply the impact and possibility you then get a number out of 25 where you can understand what I call the risk factor.

More and more governments and institutions are taking away our need for thinking about risk by always giving warnings. But dumbing down our abilities is not the way to go! Risk does not seem to be taught very well in schools either. However, understanding and being able to deal with risk effectively and efficiently is a major factor in reaching the Advanced Power State.

CHAPTER 16

Structured Problem Solving

Problem solving is another essential skill in reaching the Advanced Power State. This skill, I am happy to say, is taught in schools, however, usually not in enough depth.

I mentioned earlier that I do not have problems and I reframe potential problems as something positive. However, there is a need to take these opportunities and work through to likely root causes so that you can then effectively deal with the root causes.

The steps are therefore quite straightforward:

- Clearly write the problem down and what the end result will look like once it has been solved
- Brainstorm by asking 'Why?' continuously 5 times on each idea.
- Analyse the results and determine the root cause(s). They will appear more than once in the roots of your work.
- Generate ideas on how to solve the root cause(s) by continually asking 'How?'
- Ascertain the best idea
- Then plan
- Execute
- Review the outcome

Have you noticed that the above is based on V.A.P.E.R?

- Vision(goal)
- Analysis
- Planning
- Execution
- Review

Vision
Clearly write down the problem and what a good result will be. What would you like the situation to be if all goes well?

Firstly define the problem you are trying to solve. Be able to clearly state the problem in writing, perhaps even write it down. Is it the real problem? Try and work out what it would be like if you did not have this problem. What would be the ideal situation?

Analysis
Take the problem, written down at the Vision stage, and ask 'Why is this the case?' 'What is causing this?' and then write the answer down. Then take that answer and ask the same questions again 'What is causing this?' 'Why is this the case?' and for each of the questions write down the answers starting with 'because…'. If you do this five times or as many times as you can, you will get to some 'tails'. When you have done this sufficiently you will have many 'tails' and you will start seeing patterns appearing with repetition.

Analyse the results and determine the root cause(s).

It is these patterns and repetitions that are the most likely root causes. Collect the number of times the same things appear or the similar branches, and you will have the starting point for generating ideas as to solving the 'problem'.

Generate ideas on how to solve the root cause(s) by continually asking 'How?'

Once you have the root causes, then it is essential to write them down clearly. A quick check back at your problem might well validate further those root causes and you can choose which ones to generate ideas on how to put them right. Keep asking yourself how can you stop this, or how you can change this, or how you can deal with this? These ideas allow you to understand the possible actions you can take.

Ascertain the best ideas.

It is then worth evaluating those ideas which will deliver the best results for the lowest effort, or in the shortest time. It is up to you to decide what action to take.

Plan
Once you have decided the action to take then it is a case of planning how you are going to achieve dealing with the problem.

Execute the plan
Once the plan is in place you need to take action. Remember: successful people take action, while others just think they should.

Review the outcome
Finally, review the outcome. Has it had the expected result? If not, go back and look at your workings. It is likely you will

understand where your thinking went wrong and try again.

Problem solving is essential. The above approach is one generic approach which is easy to understand and worth using. However, go out and research using different approaches.

CHAPTER 17

Structured Decision Making

Decision making is also essential in reaching the Advanced Power State. We make decisions all of the time but what is the quality of those decisions? As with many other things, decision-making is based on sound judgement coming from Knowledge and Experience.

Someone capable of reaching the Advanced Power State would realize that along with action comes decision making, and it is those people who fail to make decisions that are almost always left behind.

Make decisions quickly but effectively and take action. Lead yourself to success.

Here is a generic way of dealing with decisions:

- Identify the decision to be made and what you want to achieve
- Carry out preliminary research into the subject
- Evaluate an effective course of action
- Research on the course of action and assess risk
- Decide and commit to do it
- Do it and continue to review

Again the process above is based on V.A.P.E.R:

- Vision (goals)
- Analysis
- Planning
- Execution
- Review

Identify the decision to be made and what you want to achieve.

It is important to establish what the decision to be made is and if you are the best person to make it. Sometimes a decision is better made by someone else, especially if they have ownership and a better understanding. You need to assess this and understand what you are trying to achieve by making the decision. This goal is again a vital part of the process.

Carry out preliminary research into the subject.

It is easy to say research the subject and in many cases you will already have what you need in your mind and may need no more information, but if you do need more, then get more:

- Ask an expert
- Look up the information on the Internet
- Read up on the subject
- Talk to someone who has done it before

There are many ways but if you do not have enough information to make a good decision then research.

Evaluate an effective course of action.

If the decision is about having multiple courses of action, then evaluate the different courses. Carry out a 'What if?' scenario. Take the course and ask 'What if I did that?' What would be the result? Brainstorm the result on a Mind Map. If you try all of the options then you will have a clearer understanding of the best way forward.

Research on the course of action and assess risk.

Once you have decided the most likely course of action then it may need to be researched further. Has anyone else done this in the past? What happened when they did it? In reality again this is often known up front.

Decide and commit to do it.

Do it!

Nike used to have a strapline with their advertising "Just do it'. At this point, once the decision has been made 'Nike' – Just do it.

Review.

Review is an essential part of managing anything. If something is not working or is having an opposite effect, then go back. Understand where your thinking was flawed and change your mind. Change it to move forward positively and understand how it is moving forward. Do not change it for the sake of it.

CHAPTER 18

Leading in the 21st Century

Ultimately there are leaders and there are followers. Those that reach the Advanced Power State will be leaders. This book would therefore not be complete without a chapter on leadership. Leadership has been written about by many people and my suggestion is you continue to read up on leadership and especially seek out autobiographies of good leaders. Take from these leaders' ideas, ideas that will help you to succeed further.

Leadership is about getting people to do things for you that they would not normally do, guiding people together to achieve the objectives that you subscribe to, that you want them to achieve.

Leadership is all about dealing with people, something we know is imperative in life. Your goals can only be achieved by dealing with others. At executive level, almost 100% of the time, you do not do anything except get on with people and motivate them to achieve the set objectives. To be a high-flier and to reach the Advanced Power State, you must be able to motivate and get people working for you, get people doing things the way you want them to.

In my experience, people have a huge untapped amount of knowledge and experience. As a leader it is up to you to get the most out of everyone you are leading. Often their knowledge and experience, their talents, are unknown, they remain hidden. Do you know the interests and past experience of the people who work with you or the people whom you lead? That experience and knowledge could be useful in the work you are doing. Without drawing it out, that knowledge, that experience, may never come out.

But leadership is nothing if it is not about achieving results by working with other people. We must therefore tap into the abilities and talents of everyone in the team. Their capability, singularly and together with your input, will define how successful your leadership is.

There are many different types of leaders. The ones that reach the Advanced Power State are leaders that live by a set of firm values.

Value based leadership

If we analyse any organisation, it can be clearly seen that everything flows from leadership.

All organisations need leaders and it is the only way to be successful. Without leaders there is no direction and no cohesion to the company or organisation.

Leadership in the Advanced Power State is built on a firm foundation of values and principles. I would hope that the values that leadership is built upon are positive but there have been many examples where the values of a leader have been unacceptable to society. Nevertheless, they have still been good leaders.

The words, values and principles, are interpreted in many different ways. When discussing Value Based Leadership, a value is an axiom you live by, something you believe, something you value, and it forms the fundamental basis behind your decision making. Values are defined and built in by you. Principles, on the other hand are different. Principles:

• Exist and are true whether you know about them or not
• Are independent of you
• Do not change over time

A principle will always apply whereas a value (unless also a principle) will not necessarily be always true. It is you that confirms the value in your own mind. It is you that decide to live by it.

Values you set yourself to live by should, however, be consistent and should not be changed. They may evolve over time but you should stick by them.

During the eighties Margaret Thatcher was the prime minister and you could see that whilst not everything she did was right, the things she did, her actions, were based on her fundamental values. She used to declare she believed in a 'property owning democracy'. John Smith, Labour, also had his own set of values and everything was driven from those values.

For a leader to be effective, they need to have values and get others in the team to believe in the values and the vision for the team. The vision will give you the goal and objectives whilst the values will represent how those objectives are reached. If others share the values and can share the objectives, the team will be successful and there will be greater energy and enthusiasm.

There is a book written by John Adair about principle centred leadership and some of what I prescribe here agrees with the foundations within that book. It is worth reading.

Values and principles are not about words but are demonstrated by:

- What we do
- How we do it
  a) Body language
  b) Verbal
  c) Visual
  d) Other signs
- Why we do it
  – Reasons behind the actions
- When we do it
- What we don't do and say

Examples of personal values

- Things are done without the expectation of reward
- Treat others with respect and kindness
- People work harder and respect something they have ownership for

Values can also be about or based on:

- Integrity
- Respect
- Tolerance
- Empathy
- Honesty

- Openness
- Kindness
- Benevolence
- Friendliness
- Caring
- Compassion
- Fairness
- Assertive not aggressive behaviour
- Supportiveness
- Proactivity

The success equation

We have already discussed the success equation:

$$DxExE(K+\chi E)T = Success$$

To be a successful leader you must therefore harness the above in the people you are leading. If you add time to the above equation you start to get work done.

A leader must focus on motivation as motivation increases available energy and affects enthusiasm.

A leader must focus on what is possible not on just what needs to be done, leaving the status quo behind.

Leaders:

- Find good resources
- Work communications well
- Create understanding

- Make decisions
- Motivate people

Find resources
Leaders find resources based on the above equation and people with true ability, a good aptitude and a positive attitude: the three As.

In a work environment, with colleagues, as with your friends, choose them carefully, where you can. Make sure that you find the right person for the job and culture. Work that little bit longer and harder to find the right person! If you make a mistake, realise it quickly and deal with it.

Work communications
Communication is probably the biggest cause of failure on the planet. You will never get your communication 100% right but the better the two-way communication is, the more likely you will achieve success. The more you, as a leader, are in tune with, and understand the people who work for you, the more likely you will achieve your objectives, and more efficiently and effectively.

Work communication encompasses many different aspects such as:

- Email
- Written reports
- Meetings
- Management information systems
- Verbal discussion in ad hoc meetings
- Verbal discussions over the telephone
- Body language

The fundamental skill that a leader can develop is that of feedback. Understand the messages coming back, learn to read the body language, ask questions that confirm understanding and take any feedback mechanism available to you. Adjust your communications accordingly.

Create understanding

Understanding is brought about by investment in time and energy to explain not only the fact but the underlying vision and personal values. With understanding comes a greater commitment and more enthusiasm. Thirty years ago people did not need to understand and would just take orders. These days people need to understand and they need to agree and buy into whatever you are doing.

Make decisions

A major part of being a leader is the power to make decisions. Remember decisions are based on your Personal Knowledge Base. Input of information and the ability to make that decision and often to take a risk are critical. This was covered in a section on decision making earlier in the book. It is an important part of leadership.

Motivate people

This is another area covered earlier in the book. It is essential that you have a strong skill in this area. It is only by working with and through people that you, as a leader, will be able to achieve your results. Leaders work in three dimensions of motivation:

- Physical
- Logical
- Emotional

Physical is where leaders get down to work with the team. They will work with their followers physically taking part and bringing in the results together. Leading into battle!

Logical comes back to a strong explainable basis behind their vision, values and principles. They can rationalise what they are doing and why they are doing it and perhaps more importantly why it makes sense to people.

And then linking these two together with the final dimension which is emotion.

Winning the hearts and minds of people is so important. Barking orders just does not work anymore in the long term. This is about getting people behind you and moving forward together.

Facilitators
Some people describe leaders as facilitators. For me, this is not the case. However, like a facilitator, they need to have a good information gathering processes. They need to have their 'feelers' out everywhere but that is where the likeness ends. Leaders need to collect information and bring lots of bits of this information from many places to the table.

Leaders need to be strong in their skill and ability to analyse, interpret and process all information quickly and accurately, and to look beyond that information by drawing out the main elements

Leaders must always keep their focus on the purpose, the vision, and on the horizon. They must be proactive and not procrastinate, something we can all do if given the chance.

As discussed before, successful people, and that includes leaders, are only good leaders if they can make decisions and take action!

Good leaders understand the basics of management and V.A.P.E.R, Vision (goals) Analysis, Planning, Execution and Review.

They are people who can release the untapped resource in others, whether that is knowledge, experience or particular talents.

Leaders use all of their personal powers to create the result. Those who reach the Advanced Power State are those that will become successful leaders.

The character of a leader

An Advanced Power State leader is:

- Charismatic
- Enthusiastic
- Dynamic
- Intelligent
- Thoughtful
- Professional
- Disciplined
- Optimistic
- Passionate
- Thorough
- A Good follower
- A guide
- Innovative

Charismatic
You will always feel you want to follow a good leader. There will be a charismatic, a caring, and a strong role model to follow. A good leader will just ooze this charismatic energy which will primarily come from vision, confidence and enthusiasm.

Enthusiastic
They will be the 'happy-go-lucky type', although they will not believe in luck, just the philosophy that luck is preparedness and opportunity coming together.

Expect the best, plan for the worst! Something a good leader always considers.

Dynamic
A leader will have plenty of energy and their own motivation. They will be the type that wants to get the job done, the type that does not just want to talk about it. They tend not to be characters that concentrate on money. Their reward is usually the success of the job.

Intelligent
An above average intelligence is needed with leadership. This is important so that leaders can keep up with their team members. The team leaders must be able to adequately communicate with all levels of person.

Thoughtful
A leader is someone who will remember the small things in life. They will remember to give you the praise and the support at the times you need it. They will remember your anniversary because they know these things are important to you.

A leader will be able to get on with others with wit and charm; they will be honest and sincere. They will be frank but tactful with it. They will have empathy.

Professional
A leader will always believe in themselves. They will have overwhelming confidence and discipline.

They will understand that discipline leads to success.

The true professional will carry on no matter how bad or good they may feel. They understand they must continue and get the job done or have additional plans to help in circumstances in which they cannot achieve.

A leader will be professional and will gain credibility through confidence and proven experience.

A professional leader will always go the extra mile.

Disciplined
A leader will always have self-discipline.

They will not have to be constantly chased up. They will run a strict time management system.

They will not be the kind of person who cuts corners. They will understand that cutting corners eventually shows as quality suffers.

Optimistic
An effective leader will be a positive person and an optimistic person. They will work on the basis of expecting the best but being aware of the worst.

They will look on the bright side and they will have trust in their team members. They will not be moaners. When people get on their case in a political way they will ignore comments and move on, or if the political difficulties are getting in the way of achieving results they will deal with them swiftly and fairly.

Thorough
An effective leader will not take shortcuts. They will realise the importance of detail and ensure that the detail is uncovered, assessed and fed in to realise the objective.

Good followers
Leaders have proven themselves as great followers first. Only by being able to follow can they lead effectively.

A guide
Teaching and learning are vital aspects of being a leader. A leader must work to develop his/her team members. Without the development, the opportunity to evolve as a team and to respond to a leader's wishes become diminished. Learning allows team members to become empowered.

Empowerment is only achieved by having:

- The Personal Knowledge Base
- The courage
- The authority
- The trust

Training is carried out by many but leaders and empowerment can be developed through this training and through mentoring.

Leaders must consider the teaching of the skill and the principle rather than just teaching the knowledge.

Leaders remember that education is also about altering behaviour patterns.

A leader will ensure that when teaching and learning goes on there is:

- Fairness
- Respecting a person
- Respecting their abilities
- Bringing them in
- Getting their skills involved
- No open criticism

Innovation

Innovation is another important characteristic of a leader. A leader is about moving forward and good ideas and innovation enable the process of moving from the status quo. I expect the Advanced Power State leaders to show considerable innovation in everything they do.

The Difference between a manager and a leader

The difference between a manager and a leader on the surface seems very little, but deep down there are fundamental differences in philosophy and role.

What is the role of a manager?

- To look after a situation
- To manage a team to achieve the aims and objectives set

A manager therefore tends to look after an existing situation. They do not generally pick up a new idea and run with it. They are not required to create and run with their own vision. They are following other's visions.

Leadership is a level above management. A leader must have and know the skills to be a good manager.

Leaders take on new situations, they work into the unknown. They create their own vision and develop their own plans to reach the vision. A leader constantly challenges the status quo. Leadership is above, leading change.

A manager takes a given vision and often key milestones and works toward the vision. They have only a limited ability to alter the chosen method and usually no ability to affect the vision.

One of the big drawbacks with managers these days is that business has become dynamic. Things do change and change quickly and vision has to be amended and steps to reach the vision adapted. Managers are not visionaries and they have limited abilities in the vision and adapting skills. Things tend to stay as the status quo. This will cause slippage in any industry in today's fast moving world.

> *I once heard the difference between management and leadership defined as 'using a compass rather than a road map'.*

A leader follows the route he/she needs to and a manager follows a road map.

Team work

A leader is totally at the mercy of their ability to make the team perform to their will. Without the performance from the whole team, success will be compromised.

A leader remembers the small things:

> *I once heard that President Bush Senior shook hands with every member of the White House. He knew the importance of such things.*

A leader identifies and analyses their own team members' strengths and weaknesses. They then work to obtain the optimum from the strengths, continuing to strengthen them, and develop the weaknesses where possible or plug the weaknesses if not possible.

A leader must ensure their team has respect for them. They need to know their team well.

They need to understand the drivers behind each member of the team to be able to motivate them and work effectively.

A leader ensures that a team has a clear agreed vision and set of objectives.

A leader must ensure they bring people into the team. They need to be able to effect a behavioural change on someone to ensure they work with them. Now it may be subtle but there is always a behavioural change, perhaps by mentoring or with some of the techniques used in the motivation chapter.

A leader is someone who has reached the Advanced Power State.

SECTION 4

Summary

Summary

This book has shown you the way to reach the Advanced Power State. It has given you the different tools and techniques and it is now up to you to play with them and build yourself towards success.

As always, if you ignore the ideas or cannot see beyond where you are now, it is going to be very difficult to change, so decide now to embrace change and spend the time to achieve the Advanced Power State. I have had people question me, asking how will they know if they have got there, to success. The answer is: you will know!

If nothing else, I hope the book has provoked some thoughts, and that you have taken at least a few of the ideas and started to use them. If that is the case, then the book has been a success.

Good luck with your success. I know that you can achieve it.